D0424596

# HONG KONG
## ENCOUNTER

**STEVE FALLON**

Hong Kong Encounter
1st edition – May 2007

Published by Lonely Planet Publications Pty Ltd
ABN 36 005 607 983

| | |
|---|---|
| Australia | Head Office, Locked Bag 1, Footscray, Vic 3011 ☎ 03 8379 8000 fax 03 8379 8111 talk2us@lonelyplanet.com.au |
| USA | 150 Linden St, Oakland, CA 94607 ☎ 510 893 8555 toll free 800 275 8555 fax 510 893 8572 info@lonelyplanet.com |
| UK | 72–82 Rosebery Avenue, Clerkenwell, London EC1R 4RW ☎ 020 7841 9000 fax 020 7841 9001 go@lonelyplanet.co.uk |

This title was commissioned in Lonely Planet's Melbourne office and produced by: **Commissioning Editor** Rebecca Chau **Coordinating Editors** Victoria Harrison, Phillip Tang **Coordinating Cartographer** Owen Eszeki **Layout Designer** Clara Monitto **Assisting Editors** Justin Flynn, Emma Gilmour, Kate James, Laura Stansfeld **Assisting Cartographers** Ross Butler, Kusnandar, Erin McManus, David Connolly **Managing Editor** Imogen Bannister **Senior Editor** Helen Christinis **Managing Cartographer** Julie Sheridan **Cover Designer** Nic Lehman **Project Manager** Eoin Dunlevy **Series Designers** Nic Lehman, Wendy Wright **Thanks to** Amanda Canning, Carlos Solarte, Celia Wood, Chris Lee Ark, David Burnett, Jim Hsu, Kate McDonald, Laura Jane, Mark Germanchis, Michelle Glynn, Pam Plaia, Sally Darmady, Stephanie Pearson, Vivek Wagle, Wayne Murphy

ISBN 978 1 74104 575 8

Printed through Colorcraft Ltd. Hong Kong.
Printed in China

**Acknowledgement** Hong Kong MTR System Map ©2006 MTR Corporation

# HOW TO USE THIS BOOK

## Colour-Coding & Maps

Colour-coding is used for symbols on maps and in the text that they relate to (eg all eating venues on the maps and in the text are given a green fork symbol). Each neighbourhood also gets its own colour, and this is used down the edge of the page and throughout that neighbourhood section.

## Prices

Multiple prices with reviews (eg $10/5/25) usually indicate adult/concession/family admission to a venue. Concession prices can include senior, student, member or coupon discounts. Meal cost categories are listed on the Quick Reference page on the inside front cover.

**Send us your Feedback** We love to hear from readers – your comments help make our books better. We read every word you send us, and we always guarantee that your feedback goes straight to the appropriate authors. The most useful submissions are rewarded with a free book. To send us your updates and find out about Lonely Planet events, newsletters and travel news – visit our award-winning website: *lonelyplanet.com/contact*.

Note: We may edit, reproduce and incorporate your comments in Lonely Planet products such as guidebooks, websites and digital products, so let us know if you don't want your comments reproduced or your name acknowledged. For a copy of our privacy policy visit *lonelyplanet.com/privacy*.

## STEVE FALLON

A native of Boston, Massachusetts, Steve graduated from Georgetown University with a Bachelor of Science in modern languages, including Chinese. After he had worked for several years for an American daily newspaper and earned a master's degree in journalism, his fascination with the 'new' Asia led him to Hong Kong, where he lived for over a dozen years, working for a variety of media and running his own travel bookshop. Steve is now based in London and gets back to Hong Kong annually.

He has written or contributed to more than two dozen Lonely Planet titles, including *Hong Kong & Macau* and *China*.

## STEVE'S THANKS

Thanks again to Margaret Leung for her hospitality and support, to James Lee for his skill with a Chinese typewriter and to Neva Shaw for, well, coming back. We missed you. As always, I'd like to dedicate my efforts to my partner, Michael Rothschild, who allows scarcely a day to go by without giving our 'hometown' a passing thought.

**Our Readers** Many thanks to the travellers who wrote to us with helpful hints, useful advice and interesting anecdotes. Noah Mccormack

**Photographs** by Michael Coyne/Lonely Planet Images p8, p11, p12, p17, p24, p6, p175, p27, p32, p34, p46, p48, p86, p131, p38; Olive Strewe/Lonely Planet Images p10, p164, p166, p167, p33, p64, p151, p154; Holger Leue p13, p90, p108, p126; Greg Elms/Lonely Planet Images p14, p20, p23, p4, p6, p177, p178, p69, p92, p107, p118, p159, p160; Phil Weymouth/Lonely Planet Images p22, p34, p78, p96, p114, p133, p134, p138, p140; Dallas Stribley/Lonely Planet Images p16, 29, 31; John Hay/Lonely Planet Images p165, p168, p174, p36, p54, p60, p71, p72, p101; Richard I'Anson/Lonely Planet Images p21, p144; Frank Carter/Lonely Planet Images p28, p149; Jon Davison p156; Lee Foster/Lonely Planet Images p179; Andrew Burke/Lonely Planet Images p18; Krysztof Dydynski/Lonely Planet Images p25; Michael Taylor/Lonely Planet Images p170; Michael Aw/Lonely Planet Images p173; Ray Laskowitz/Lonely Planet Images p177; Izzet Zeribar/Lonely Planet Images p89; James Marshall/Lonely Planet Images p122; So Hing-Keung/Corbis p30; EPA p26; Steve Fallon p53, p77, p83, p102, 125. **Cover photograph** Shoppers walk under bird cages decoration at a shopping mall in Hong Kong, Bobby Yip/Reuters

All images are copyright of the photographers unless otherwise indicated. Many of the images in this guide are available for licensing from **Lonely Planet Images**: www.lonelyplanetimages.com.

Passengers on the Peak Tram ascending Victoria Peak

# CONTENTS

# THIS IS HONG KONG

You're shopping for *conpoy* (that's dried scallops to the cognoscenti) at a stall draped in a red, white and blue plastic tarpaulin when a guy in an Armani suits jumps out of his Lexus and starts fingering the *maw* (fish stomach). Or perhaps it's winter and you've joined your Chinese friends with the 'tea' (bleached orange) hair on a dare for a meal of 'phoenix and dragon' (chicken and snake).

Or you might be in the bubble lift of a luxury hotel heading for your room when the tailor calls to say your suit is ready for the second fitting.

All of this and much, much more is Hong Kong – a place that is a million different things to a million different people. A pulsating, superlative-ridden fusion of West and East, an exercise in controlled chaos, a densely populated 'place that shouldn't be but is', Hong Kong is simply like no other city on earth. Shanghai might be trying to steal the limelight these days and upstart Singapore actually thinks it's in the running (bless), but Hong Kong remains the top destination in Asia for wining and dining, entertainment, shopping, accommodation and sheer unadulterated fun.

And it's a city of constant surprises. The Chinese world, with its noise, activity, unfamiliar food and language, is everywhere here, but intruding into this sphere are familiar icons – monolithic skyscrapers wedged between food stalls and microscopic workshops, Christian churches next to Taoist and Buddhist temples, minimalist fusion restaurants beside noodle shops. The meeting of these two worlds shakes and stirs into an invigorating cocktail of colour and aroma, taste and sensation

It's an intoxicating place, spectacular, exotic and accessible. If you're visiting for business, you'll find pleasure sneaking up on you. If you're visiting for pleasure, there are thousands of locals who make it their business to please.

---

**Top left** Practising t'ai chi (p170) **Bottom left** A dim sum diner at Lin Heung Tea House (p65) **Bottom right** Nightlife in Lan Kwai Fong

Shopping district of Causeway Bay.

# > 1 WET MARKET
## SLIP-SLIDIN' INTO THE HEART OF HONG KONG'S CUISINE

Nothing illustrates Hong Kong's zest for fresh (and, in many cases, live) food more colourfully than a wet market, so called because the ground is continually hosed down to wash away the detritus spilling from the fish, fruit and vegetable stalls. Though the government, ever vigilant against things deemed unhygienic in the wake of SARS and avian flu, has shut down many of the markets in recent years or converted them into sterile and soulless places of aluminium and white tiles, a few places carry on, including our favourite, the outdoor Graham Street Market (p64). Walk up from Queen's Rd Central (or down from Hollywood Rd) and prepare yourself for the cacophony and bustle, and the press of people lingering over, discussing and bargaining for food. Fishmongers sing out the praises of their grouper and red snapper flapping about on beds of shaved ice while greengrocers tempt shoppers by slicing open samples of their best fruit and vegetables. Ideally you'll visit a wet market with a local – how else are you going to be able to tell a star fruit from a custard apple or distinguish between preserved eggs (the ready-to-eat greenish-black ones packed in a mixture of ash, lime and salt and buried for 100 days) and bright-orange salted eggs, which are soaked in brine for 40 days and cooked before eating, usually with *congee* (rice porridge). Be warned, though: those of a squeamish disposition might find wet markets unnerving.

# >2 TRAMS

## ROCK & ROLL ALONG HONG KONG ISLAND'S NORTHERN COAST

Though there are any number of inventive ways to be shepherded around Hong Kong Island (p199), our favourite views of the northern shore are from a tram (p195). Hong Kong's venerable old trams are hardly the fastest or flashest way to go, but they're cheap and a lot of fun; in fact, apart from the Star Ferry (p192), no form of transport is nearer and dearer to the hearts of Hong Kong people. These 164 tall, narrow streetcars comprise the world's only fully double-decker tramcar fleet, and they roll (and rock) along 13km of track from Kennedy Town in the west to Shau Kei Wan in the east, carrying almost a quarter of a million passengers a day. Try to get a seat at the front window on the upper deck for a first-class view while rattling through the crowded streets. Tall passengers will find it uncomfortable standing up as the ceiling is low, but there is more space at the rear of the tram on both decks. And be prepared to elbow your way through the crowd to alight, particularly on the lower deck.

## >3 HAPPY VALLEY RACES

### A NIGHT AT THE RACES IN HAPPY VALLEY

No group of people (with the possible exception of the British) enjoys a flutter as much as the Chinese, and horse racing, worth more than US$1 billion annually, remains the most popular form of gambling in Hong Kong. Be prepared for a lot of, well, excitement (read: noise) at the races. Hong Kong Chinese view it both as a sport and a very serious way to augment their income! The first horse races were held at the Happy Valley Racecourse (p82) in 1846. Now there are about 80 meetings a year split between the racecourse here and the newer and larger (but less atmospheric) one at Sha Tin in the New Territories. The racing season runs from September to early July. If you've been in Hong Kong for less than 21 days and are over 18 years of age, you can buy a tourist ticket, which allows you to jump the queue, sit in the members' enclosure and walk around next to the finish area. Make sure to bring along your passport as proof. Another option is to join the Come Horseracing tour (p199).

# >4 PENINSULA HOTEL

### FIT FOR A TEA AT HONG KONG'S LEGENDARY HOTEL

One of the world's great hotels, the Peninsula (p115) is both a landmark and an icon of Hong Kong. Though it was being called 'the finest hotel east of Suez' a few years after opening in 1928, the Peninsula was in fact one of several prestigious hostelries across Asia where everybody who was anybody stayed, lining up with the likes of Raffles in Singapore, the Peace (then the Cathay) in Shanghai and the Strand in Rangoon (now Yangon). Taking afternoon tea at the Peninsula is one of the best experiences in town – dress neatly and be prepared to queue for a table. While you're waiting, you can listen to the string quartet and salivate at the sight of everyone else's cucumber sandwiches, scones and dainty cakes. The price of afternoon tea, served from 2pm to 7pm daily, for one – how sad! – is $238 and it's $338 a couple. It attracts a mixed clientele – from Japanese tourists to *tai tais* (any married women but especially the leisured wives of wealthy businessmen), who grab the most prominent tables, sip and gossip with their friends (mostly via mobile phones). When you're through (and to bring yourself back to earth) cross Nathan Rd and have a look round the shopping arcade of the rabbit warren called Chungking Mansions (p112).

## >5 DIM SUM

### INDULGE IN SOME YUM-YUM YUM CHA

Yum cha (literally 'drink tea') is the usual way to refer to dim sum, the uniquely Cantonese 'meal' eaten as breakfast, brunch or lunch between about 7am and 3pm. Eating dim sum is a social occasion, consisting of many separate dishes that are meant to be shared. The bigger your group, the better. Dim sum delicacies are normally steamed in small bamboo baskets. The baskets are stacked up on trolleys and rolled around the dining room. You don't need a menu (though these exist too but almost always in Chinese); just stop the waiter and choose something from the trolley. It will be marked

### TEA TOO

Choosing the tea is as important to Chinese people as selecting the dishes at yum cha. Basically there are three main types: green (or unfermented) tea *(luk cha)*; black tea *(hung cha* in Chinese, which translates as 'red tea'), which is fermented and includes the ever-popular *bole* and oolong *(wu lung cha)* tea, which is semifermented. In between are countless scented variations, such as *heung ping* (jasmine), which is a blend of black tea and flower petals. When your teapot is empty and you want a refill, signal the waiter by taking the lid off the pot and resting it on the handle.

down on a bill left on the table. Don't try to order everything at once. Each trolley has a different selection, so take your time and order as they come. It's said that there are about a thousand dim sum dishes, but you'd be doing well to sample 10 in one sitting.

*char siu bau* – steamed barbecued pork buns
*cheung fun* – steamed rice flour rolls with shrimp, beef or pork
*ching chau si choi* – fried green vegetable of the day
*chun gun* – fried spring rolls
*fan guo* – steamed dumplings with shrimp and bamboo shoots
*fu pei gun* – crispy bean-curd rolls
*fun guo* – steamed dumpling with pork, peanuts and coriander
*fung jau* – fried chicken's feet
*har gau* – steamed shrimp dumplings
*loh mei fan* – sticky rice wrapped in lotus leaf
*pai guat* – small braised spareribs with black beans
*san juk ngau yok* – steamed minced beef balls
*siu mai* – steamed pork and shrimp dumplings

Dim sum restaurants are normally brightly lit and very large and noisy – it's rather like eating in an aircraft hangar. See p167 for a list of the best.

## >6 STAR FERRY   NOV 4/08

### JUMP ABOARD FLOATING HISTORY IN VICTORIA HARBOUR

You can't say you've 'done' Hong Kong until you've taken a ride on the Star Ferry (p192), that wonderful little fleet of electric-diesel boats first launched in 1888. With names like *Morning Star, Celestial Star* and *Twinkling Star,* the ferries are most romantic at night. The boats are festively strung with lights, the city buildings beam onto the rippling water, the frenzy of Hong Kong by day has eased (somewhat) and ca-noodling appears to be the only sensible thing to do. If possible, try to take the trip on a clear night from Kowloon side to Central; it's not half as dramatic in the other direction. The trip takes about nine minutes (as long as it used to take to read the now defunct *Hong Kong Star,* a low-brow tabloid newspaper, it was said), and departures are very frequent. Indeed, morning and evening, the Star Ferry is a common way for local people to hop from island to mainland and back again.

## >7 SIK SIK YUEN WONG TAI SIN TEMPLE

**CALLING ON THE HEAVENS FROM NEW KOWLOON**

Like most Chinese Taoist temples, Sik Sik Yuen Wong Tai Sin Temple (p139) is an explosion of colour with red pillars, bright yellow roofs and green-and-blue latticework. If you visit in the late afternoon or early evening, you can watch hordes of businessmen and secretaries praying and divining the future with *chim,* bamboo 'prediction sticks' that must be shaken out of a box on to the ground and then read (they're available free to the left of the main temple). Behind the main temple and to the right are the Good Wish Gardens, replete with colourful pavilions (the hexagonal Unicorn Hall with carved doors and windows is the most beautiful), zigzag bridges and artificial ponds. Just below the main temple and to the left as you enter the complex is an arcade filled with dozens of booths operated by fortune-tellers. Some of the fortune-tellers speak decent English (and advertise the fact on signs above their counters), so if you really want to know what fate has in store for you, this is your chance. The busiest times at the temple are around the Chinese New Year, Wong Tai Sin's birthday (23rd day of the eighth month – usually in September) and at weekends, especially Friday evening.

*Peak tram*

# >8 THE PEAK

*Nov 7/08*

## A BREATH OF FRESH AIR AT THE TOP OF HONG KONG ISLAND

The Peak (p74), Hong Kong Island's highest point, has been *the* place to live ever since the British came on the scene in the 19th century. The taipans built summer houses here to escape the heat and humidity (it's usually about 5°C cooler here than down below). The Peak remains the most fashionable – and expensive – area to live in Hong Kong and is the territory's foremost tourist destination. Not only is the view from the summit one of the most spectacular cityscapes in the world, it's also a good way to get Hong Kong into perspective. And the only way up, as far as we are concerned, is via the Peak Tram (p195).

Rising above the Peak Tram terminus is the seven-storey Peak Tower, an anvil-shaped building containing shops, restaurants, an outpost of the waxworks Madame Tussaud's (p76) and a viewing terrace. Opposite is the Peak Galleria, a three-storey mall of shops and restaurants. Like the tower, it is designed to withstand winds of up to 270km/h, theoretically more than the maximum velocity of a No 10 typhoon.

When people in Hong Kong refer to the Peak, they usually mean the plateau and surrounding residential area at about 400m. The

summit, Victoria Peak (552m), is about 500m northwest of the Peak Tram terminus up steep Mt Austin Rd. The governor's mountain lodge near the summit was burned to the ground by the Japanese during WWII, but the gardens remain and are open to the public.

You can walk around Victoria Peak without exhausting yourself. Harlech Rd on the south side and Lugard Rd on the northern slope together form a 3.5km loop that takes about an hour to walk. If you feel like a longer stroll (and want to avoid the Peak Tram and its crowds on the way down), you can continue for a further 2km along Peak Rd to Pok Fu Lam Reservoir Rd, which leaves Peak Rd near the car park exit. This goes past the reservoir to the main Pok Fu Lam Rd, where you can get bus 7 back to Central. Another good walk leads down to Hong Kong University. First walk to the west side of Victoria Peak by taking either Lugard or Harlech Rds. After reaching Hatton Rd, follow it down. The descent is steep, but the path is clear.

### THE WAY UP THERE
'Removed high above the dust and noise of the town, the Peak Hotel offers the traveller those few days of quiet rest so necessary after a long sea voyage. Rates per day from $5.00 up.' From the guidebook *Hongkong and its Vicinity*, 1911

# >9 HONG KONG MUSEUM OF HISTORY

## TAKE A TRIP BACK THROUGH TIME

Commercial Hong Kong may have its eyes firmly on the future, but when you see a computer-shop owner tending a shrine to the earth god Tou Tei in his store, you get the notion that at least some of the city's character lies in its past. 'The Hong Kong Story' at the Hong Kong Museum of History (p112) takes visitors on a fascinating walk through the territory's past via eight galleries, starting with the natural environment and prehistoric Hong Kong on the ground floor – about 6000 years ago, give or take a lunar year – and ending with the territory's return to China in 1997 and a tear-jerking (well, we cried) video collage of Hong Kong through the ages on the 2nd. Along the way you'll encounter replicas of village dwellings; traditional Chinese costumes and beds; a re-creation of an entire arcaded street in Central from 1881, including an old Chinese medicine shop; a tram from 1913; and film footage of WWII, including recent interviews with Chinese and foreigners taken prisoner by the Japanese. A favourite exhibit remains the jumble of toys and collectables from the 1960s and '70s when 'Made in Hong Kong' meant 'Christmas stocking trash'. If you are like us and prefer modern history to ancient, you'll take a lift to the 2nd floor and do the exhibit backward. That way, if you run out of time, you can give all those cave dwellers and their stone ornaments a miss.

# > 10 STANLEY MARKET

## CHEAP AND CHEERFUL WITH ALL KINDS OF BARGAINS

Stanley, on Hong Kong Island's southern coast, is known for a lot of things, including its fort that became a notorious prison during WWII, its beaches and its colourful dragon boat races in June. But its real claim to fame is Stanley Market (p107) and the reason why buses 6, 6A, 6X and 260 are almost always full. The covered market that fills the alleys and lanes to the southwest of Stanley Village Rd is stuffed to the gills with bric-a-brac, cheap clothing and junk. Some people find it overrated but as Ellen McNally points out in her excellent and now fully revised *Shop in Hong Kong: A Insider's Guide* 'This market is one of the few places where you can find large sizes, fashionable cashmere sweaters at a reasonable price…well-known children's brands at greatly discounted prices [and] unique bed linens'. At the weekend – even in the rain – the market is bursting at the seams with tourists and locals alike on the prowl for bargains; if possible, schedule your visit during the week. And after you've purchased everything you really don't need, consume further at one of the attractive waterfront bars or restaurants to the east such as the Boathouse (p108).

## >11 HONG KONG PARK
### UP WITH THE BIRDS IN A ROOFTOP AVIARY

Deliberately designed to look anything but natural, Hong Kong Park (p82) is one of the most unusual parks in the world, emphasising artificial creations such as its fountain plaza, conservatory, artificial waterfall, indoor games hall, playground, t'ai chi garden, viewing tower, museums and an arts centre. For all its artifice, the eight-hectare park is beautiful in its own weird way and, with a wall of skyscrapers on one side and mountains on the other, makes for dramatic photographs. The best and liveliest feature is the Edward Youde Aviary, named after a much-loved former governor (1982–87) and China scholar who died suddenly while in office. Home to hundreds of birds representing some 150 different species, the aviary is huge and very natural-feeling. Visitors walk along a wooden bridge suspended 10m above ground, at eye level with tree branches where most of the birds are; there are about a dozen viewing platforms. Schedule your visit in the morning, when the birds are most active. Volunteers from the Hong Kong Bird Watching Society lead visitors through the park and aviary, identifying various species, including sulphur-created cockatoos, Chinese bulbuls and blue magpies.

## >12 TEMPLE STREET NIGHT MARKET
**WHERE YOU GET DINNER AND A SHOW**   *NOV 8 - kerbside shrimp were delisi!*

Temple Street, named after the temple dedicated to Tin Hau at its centre, hosts the liveliest night market (p130) in Hong Kong. It used to be known as 'Men's Street' because the market only sold men's clothing and to distinguish it from the 'Ladies Market' on Tung Choi St (p131) to the northeast. Though there are still a lot of items on sale for men, vendors don't discriminate – anyone's money will do. But don't just come here to shop; this is also a place for eating and entertainment. For street food, head for Woo Sung St, running parallel to the east, or to the section of Temple St north of the temple toward Man Ming Lane. You can get anything from a simple bowl of noodles to a full meal served at your very own kerbside table. There are a few seafood and hotpot restaurants as well or you might pop into Mido (p134), Hong Kong's best known *cha chan tang* (café with local dishes). You'll also find a surfeit of fortune-tellers and herbalists and some free, open-air Cantonese opera performances here. The market officially opens in the afternoon and closes at midnight but it is at its best from about 7pm to 10pm, when it's clogged with stalls and people. If you want to carry on, visit the colourful wholesale fruit market (corner Shek Lung and Reclamation Sts), which is always a hive of activity from midnight to dawn.

# >13 HONG KONG WETLAND PARK

## HIDES AND FEATHERS IN THE MARSHES

If you're a real bird fancier, the Mai Po Marsh, a fragile, 270-hectare ecosystem in the northwestern New Territories and one of the largest natural habitats for wildlife in Hong Kong, is the best place to meet up with thousands of your feathered friends. But it's reserved for serious aficionados and is not the easiest place to reach. The more accessible Hong Kong Wetland Park (p144) contains a huge visitor centre called Wetland Interactive World, with three major galleries and a surfeit of hands-on and educational exhibits, a theatre and a resource centre. Outside there are four brief boardwalk walking trails through marshland and mangrove swamps, complete with viewing platforms and bird hides, and a discovery centre – all in all, a kind of high-tech Mai Po Marsh. The park is also now the home of Pui Pui, the irascible pet crocodile that escaped and managed to find his way to the Shan Pui River in Yuen Long, eluding would-be captors from Hong Kong, China and Australia for seven not-so-snappy months in 2004. Pui Pui seems content in his 'furnished' tank at the start of the nature trails but, like us, is no doubt unimpressed with the backdrop of Shenzhen on the mainland belching out pollution.

# >14 HONG KONG VIEWS

## AS HIGH AS IT GETS HERE

'Hong Kong is like no other place in the world, where the East collides head on with the West' was a sentence we wrote some years back in an article that dealt with the territory as an exotic destination and it remains true today. Superlatives and clichés are – and always have been – acceptable to people in this, the world's largest Cantonese, city. Biggest, brightest and especially highest – those are the sort of things that make Hong Kong tick. To get as high as you can in Hong Kong (and we're talking lifts and elevators here), head for the Bank of China Tower (p44) designed by China-born American architect IM Pei in 1990. Take the express lift to the 43rd floor from where you'll be rewarded with a panoramic view over Hong Kong. From here you are about the same height as the Hongkong & Shanghai Bank to the northwest. It's a pity that you aren't allowed to go any higher, as it's exciting swaying with the wind at the top. Even higher (though arguably not as dramatic) is the view from the windows of the Hong Kong Monetary Authority Information Centre on the 55th floor of the Two International Finance Centre (p49). OK, the exhibits focusing on Hong Kong's currency, fiscal policy and banking history are not exactly a crowd-pleaser, but who's come all the way up here for those?

# >15 DISNEYLAND & NGONG PING VILLAGE

## WHERE BUDDHA AND MICKEY MOUSE ARE AT ONE

Much of Hong Kong is based on artifice and one of the best ways to see it at its most 'plastic' is to combine a trip to Hong Kong Disneyland (p149) with one to Ngong Ping Village (p149) via the new hair-raising Ngong Ping Skyrail (p149). To make the trip, catch the Tung Chung MTR line from Central or Kowloon and change at Sunny Bay station for Disneyland Resort. After a quick look around (that's all you'll need – it's one of the world's smallest Disney theme parks), take the MTR to Tung Chung and transfer to the Ngong Ping Skyrail, which departs from the terminus just northwest of the Tung Chung MTR station. The journey, which takes 20 to 25 minutes, offers startling (and very real) views of the airport, Tung Chung and North Lantau Country Park, and ends at Ngong Ping Village, a Chinese 'Disneyland' with multimedia attractions relating to the life of the Buddha and the Buddhist Jataka tales. Have a look at the living and fully working Po Lin Monastery immediately to the east and then catch bus 2 to Mui Wo (Silvermine Bay), where the ferry will take you back to Central (or on the weekend Tsim Sha Tsui).

# >HONG KONG DIARY

No matter what the time of year, you're almost certain to find some colourful festival or event occurring in Hong Kong. The choice seems endless – from long-established cultural events like the Hong Kong Arts Festival, now in its third decade, to the 'infant' but no less popular Hong Kong Art Walk. Major sporting events such as the Hong Kong Rugby World Cup Sevens bring excitement and the fun of competition, but nothing is as colourful as Hong Kong's traditional Chinese holidays, especially the Mid-Autumn Festival.

Mid-Autumn Festival, Victoria Park (p97), Causeway Bay

HONG KONG DIARY

# JANUARY

## Chinese New Year

www.discoverhongkong.com/eng
/heritage/festivals/index.jhtml
Southern China's most important public
holiday (pictured below) is welcomed in
by flower markets, fireworks and a huge
international parade.

## Hong Kong City Festival

www.hkfringe.com.hk
Three weeks of eclectic performances both
local and from overseas.

# FEBRUARY

## Hong Kong Arts Festival

www.hk.artsfestival.org
A month-long extravaganza of music,
performing arts and exhibitions by hundreds
of local and international artists.

## Spring Lantern Festival

www.discoverhongkong.com/eng
/heritage/festivals/Index.jhtml
This colourful lantern festival (pictured right)
on the 15th day of the first moon (mid- to
late February) marks the end of the lunar
new year period and is a day for lovers.

# MARCH

### Hong Kong Art Walk
www.hongkongartwalk.com
More than 40 galleries throw open their doors.

### Hong Kong Rugby World Cup Sevens www.hksevens.com.hk
This seven-a-side tournament attracts teams and spectators from all over the world.

### Man Hong Kong International Literary Festival
www.festival.org.hk
Features novelists, short story writers and poets from around the region and world.

# APRIL

### Ching Ming
www.discoverhongkong.com/eng /heritage/festivals/index.jhtml
A family celebration when people visit and clean the graves of ancestors.

### Hong Kong International Film Festival
www.hkiff.org.hk
Screenings of almost 250 films from 40 countries worldwide.

### Birthday of Tin Hau
www.discoverhongkong.com/eng /heritage/festivals/index.jhtml
This festival honours the patroness of sailors and fisherfolk — one of the territory's most popular goddesses.

### Cheung Chau Bun Festival
www.cheungchau.org
This is an unusual festival involving buns (p148) that is observed uniquely on Cheung Chau.

HONG KONG DIARY

# MAY

### Birthday of Lord Buddha

www.discoverhongkong.com/eng
/heritage/festivals/index.jhtml
On this public holiday, Buddha's statue is
taken from monasteries and temples and
ceremonially bathed in scented water.

# JUNE

### Dragon Boat Festival

www.discoverhongkong.com/eng
/heritage/festivals/index.jhtml
This festival commemorates the death of
a 3rd-century-BC poet-statesman who
hurled himself into a river to protest against
a corrupt government. Dragon boat races
(pictured above) are held throughout the
territory but the most famous are at Stanley.

# JULY

## Hong Kong Fashion Week for Spring/Summer

http://hkfashionweekss.tdctrade.com

This is the spring-summer section of the biannual Hong Kong Fashion week. The week for fall-winter is held in January.

## MOVEABLE FEASTS

Many Chinese red-letter days, both public holidays and privately observed affairs, go back hundreds, even thousands, of years, and the true origins of some are often lost in the mists of time. Dates vary from year to year, so if you want to time your visit to coincide with a particular event, check the website of the **Hong Kong Tourism Board** (www.discoverhongkong.com). In modern day Hong Kong there's a festival for everything: film and the arts, salsa, winter, all things French, Italian, Spanish and Mexican — even shopping gets its own spot on the calendar.

# AUGUST

## Hungry Ghost Festival

www.discoverhongkong.com/eng/heritage/festivals/index.jhtml

Marks the day when the gates of hell are opened and restless spirits are freed for two weeks to walk the earth. Paper 'hell' money and votives in the shape of cars, houses and clothing are burned (pictured left) on the last day.

# SEPTEMBER

## Mid-Autumn Festival

www.discoverhongkong.com/eng
/heritage/festivals/index.jhtml

Held on the 15th night of the eighth moon
(sometime in September or October), this
colourful festival (pictured left) involves
eating little round 'moon' cakes while
gazing at the full moon.

# OCTOBER

## Cheung Yeung

www.discoverhongkong.com/eng
/heritage/festivals/index.jhtml

This festival is based on a Han dynasty story,
where an oracle advised a man to take his
family to a high place to escape a plague.
Many people still head for the hills on this
day and also visit the graves of ancestors.

# NOVEMBER

## Hong Kong International
## Cricket Sixes

www.hksixes.com

This two-day tournament pits Hong Kong's
top cricketers against select teams from the
eight Test-playing nations,

# ITINERARIES

## ONE DAY

Catch the Peak Tram up to the Peak (p74) for fine views of the city and a morning constitutional along the summit's circular path. Back down at sea level take a stroll through Hong Kong Park (p82) before taking a tea break at the Lock Cha Tea Shop (p52) in the KS Lo Gallery. A lift in the Island Shangri-La Hong Kong Hotel will take you down to Pacific Place (p80) for some shopping. Later cross over into Wan Chai for a drink at Maya (p91) and then board a tram to Causeway Bay for sushi at WasabiSabi (p100).

## TWO DAYS

If your stay in Hong Kong amounts to a weekend, on day two take the Star Ferry (p192) to Tsim Sha Tsui and visit the Hong Kong Museum of History (p112). Meander over to Nathan Rd for some dim sum at Wu Kong Shanghai Restaurant (p123) and then do some shopping along the so-called Golden Mile, until you're ready for afternoon tea at the Peninsula Hotel (p115). Wander up to Yau Ma Tei and the Jade Market (p130). A mere hop, skip and slip northeast is Temple St night market (p130) where you can sample street food, have your fortune told and, if lucky, catch some open-air Cantonese opera.

## THREE DAYS

On the third day, wander around Central and Sheung Wan, poking your head into traditional shops (p48). The Macau Ferry Terminal is just across the road; why not hop aboard? Have lunch at the Clube Militar de Macau (p157) before visiting the embarrassment of sights and attractions around the Largo do Senado (p155) or trying your luck at the new Wynn Macau Casino (p159). Walk along Rua Central through much of the Unesco-listed 'Historic Centre of Macau' (p154) and finish with a meal at Restaurante Litoral (p158). Back in Hong Kong spend the evening carousing in Lan Kwai Fong (p66).

---

**Top left** Eu Yan Sang (p59), traditional medicine shop, Soho **Top right** Cat St market (p44), Sheung Wan **Bottom** A café in the Peak Tower (p78) **Previous Page** Largo do Senado (p155), Macau.

ITINERARIES

Hong Kong's Zoological and Botanical Gardens (p45)

## OPEN ALL HOURS

Let's say you had a late night – er, a very early morning – and missed your flight, and now you have an extra day. What's left of it, that is. Go for a work-out and sauna at Pure Fitness (p73) or, if you're feeling a bit more passive, visit Happy Foot Reflexology Centre (p72). Afterwards, enjoy a cup of coffee and some live music at Joyce Is Not Here (p72). The Hong Kong Zoological & Botanical Gardens (p45) are open late; why not watch someone else make a monkey of themselves? Have a quiet drink at the Fringe Club (p71) and an early night.

## ISLAND ESCAPADE

Hong Kong's crowds – everywhere at all times and always directly in your path – can be a real downer. Escape them by fleeing to Lantau: take the MTR to Tung Chung and board the Ngong Ping Skyrail (p149) to Ngong Ping and the Tian Tan Buddha (p149). After a vegetarian lunch at the canteen of Po Lin Monastery (p150) board bus 21 for the traditional village of Tai O (p148). Bus 1 will return you to Mui Wo (Silvermine Bay) and the ferry to Central. Along the way, get off at Upper Cheung Sha beach (p148) for a swim or stroll.

## FOR FREE

When the only thing in your pocket is 'shrapnel' (the little brown coins that make up $1), don't despair. Admission to places like the Flagstaff House Museum of Tea Ware (p82) in Hong Kong Park and the Hong Kong Heritage Discovery Centre in Kowloon Park (p115) is always gratis, but Wednesday is 'admission free' day at six museums: Hong Kong Heritage Museum (p144), Hong Kong Museum of Art (p112), Hong Kong Museum of Coastal Defence (p97), Hong Kong Museum of History (p112), Hong Kong Science Museum (p113) and Hong Kong Space Museum (p113), excluding the Space Theatre. For something more dramatic, head for the public viewing deck at the Bank of China (p44).

### FORWARD PLANNING

**Three weeks before you go** Check out some of the key Hong Kong websites (p197); get to know what's going on – both in the headlines and after hours – online by reading the local media (p194); check to see if your visit coincides with any major holidays or festivals (p27); make sure your passport and other documents are in order.

**One week before you go** Book tickets for any major concerts or shows that might interest you at places like Hong Kong City Hall (p55), the Hong Kong Cultural Centre (p126), or the Fringe Club (p71); book a table at Petrus (p88) or M at the Fringe (p65); remind your mother that she promised to feed the cat during your absence.

**The day before you go** Reconfirm your flight; check the Hong Kong websites for any last-minute changes or cancellations at entertainment venues; buy some Hong Kong dollars; cancel the milk.

A Lockhart Rd tea house, Wan Chai

# NEIGHBOURHOODS

Hong Kong is made up of four main areas: Hong Kong Island to the south; the Kowloon peninsula across the harbour to the north; the New Territories, which sprawl northward from Kowloon to mainland China; and the 234 Outlying Islands. A percentage of Hong Kong is actually built on reclaimed land. In fact, over the past four decades, Hong Kong's surface area has grown some 7% – from 1032 sq km to 1104 sq km – due to this land 'reclamation'.

Central, on Hong Kong Island's northern shore and mostly built on reclaimed land, is a centre for sightseeing, business, transport and, in Soho and Lan Kwai Fong, wining and dining. To the west is more traditional Sheung Wan, and rising above it are the Mid-Levels residential area and the Peak. To the east of Central is Admiralty, a clump of office towers, hotels and shopping malls; Wan Chai, once a seedy red-light district but now a popular entertainment district; and frantic Causeway Bay, the most popular shopping area on the island. Further east are the various districts of Island East. Island South is home to Stanley and its famous market; Repulse Bay and its beach; and Aberdeen, Hong Kong's original settlement.

Across Victoria Harbour is Kowloon – its epicentre, the shopping and entertainment district of Tsim Sha Tsui, also reclaimed land. To the north are the working-class areas of Yau Ma Tei and Mong Kok, a sometimes seedy district that is being spruced up. Beyond is New Kowloon with everything from the cheapest computers in Hong Kong to the largest temple complex.

The New Territories is a mixed bag of congested 'New Towns', such as Sha Tin, and some surprisingly unspoiled areas like Sai Kung East Country Park and the protected Mai Po Marsh. Most of Hong Kong's 294 islands are inaccessible, but those that can be reached by public ferry include Cheung Chau, with its traditional village and fishing fleet, Lamma, which is famed for its restaurants, and Lantau, which has excellent beaches and trails.

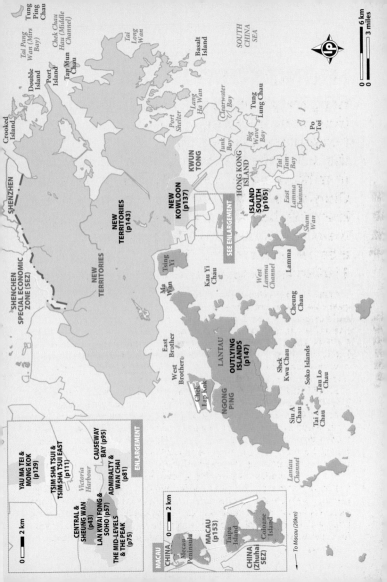

# >HONG KONG ISLAND: CENTRAL & SHEUNG WAN

All visitors to Hong Kong will inevitably pass through Central – whether it be for sightseeing, taking care of errands such as changing money or buying plane tickets, or boarding or getting off the Airport Express to/from Hong Kong International Airport at Chek Lap Kok. As Hong Kong's business centre, Central has some impressive architectural treasures that can be quite magnificent, especially at night. Though Hong Kong has always been less than sentimental about its past, there's an eclectic assortment of historical civic buildings and churches in the district. Parks, gardens and other green 'lungs' help to round out the picture. Sheung Wan isn't quite the echo of 'old Shanghai' that it was a few years back, but traditional shops and old 'ladder streets' (steep inclined streets with steps) cling on. Hollywood Rd, especially its western end, is an interesting street to explore.

## CENTRAL & SHEUNG WAN

### 👁 SEE
Bank of China Tower ....... **1** D1
Cat St Market.................. **2** B5
Center............................. **3** B3
Exchange Square........... **4** B2
Former French Mission
Building.......................... **5** D2
Government House ......... **6** D2
Hong Kong Planning &
Infrastructure Exhibition
Gallery ............................ **7** C1
Hong Kong Zoological &
Botanical Gardens........... **8** D3
Hongkong & Shanghai
Bank ............................... **9** C2
Jardine House............... **10** C2
Legislative Council
Building....................... **11** C2
Man Mo Temple ........... **12** B4
One International
Finance Centre ............ **13** B3
Para/Site Art Space ...... **14** B5

St John's Cathedral........ **15** D2
Statue Square................ **16** C2
Two International
Finance Centre ............ **17** B2
Western Market ............ **18** A4

### 🛍 SHOP
Blanc de Chine............... **19** C2
Fook Ming Tong Tea
Shop.............................. **20** B2
Hanart TZ Gallery .......... **21** C2
Hong Kong Book
Centre............................ **22** C2
IFC Mall......................... **23** B2
Joyce.............................. **24** C3
King Fook Jewellery ...... **25** C3
Liuligongfang ............... **26** C2
Lock Cha Tea Shop........ **27** B4
Shanghai Tang .............. **28** C3
Toy Museum ................. **29** C2

### 🍴 EAT
City Hall Maxim's
Palace ............................ **30** C1
City'super ..................... **31** B2
Hunan Garden .............. **32** B2
Katong........................... **33** B4
Korea House .................. **34** A4
Leung Hing
Restaurant .................... **35** A5

### 🍸 DRINK
Captain's Bar ................ **36** C2

### ⭐ PLAY
California Fitness .......... **37** C3
Hong Kong City Hall ...... **38** C1
Palace IFC Cinema ........ **39** B2
Pure Fitness.................. **40** B2

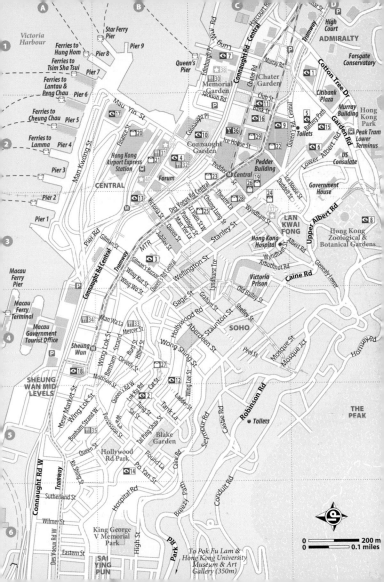

# ◉ SEE

## ◎ BANK OF CHINA TOWER
中國銀行大廈

**1 Garden Rd, Central; admission free;** ⏰ **8am-6pm Mon-Fri;** Ⓜ **Central (exit J2)**

This stunning, 70-storey structure is currently Hong Kong's third-tallest building. The asymmetry of the structure is simply geometric exercise. Rising from the ground like a cube, it is successively reduced, quarter by quarter, until the south-facing side is left to rise upward on its own. The views from the 43rd floor are stunning (p178).

## ◎ CAT ST MARKET
摩囉街

**Upper Lascar Row, Sheung Wan;** ⏰ **10am-6pm;** 🚌 **26**

Upper Lascar Row, the official name of what has become known as Cat St, is a pedestrian-only laneway lined with antique and curio shops and stalls selling found objects, cheap jewellery, ornaments, carvings and newly minted 'antique' coins. It's a fun place to trawl through for a trinket or two, but expect a lot of rough, and few (if any) diamonds.

## ◎ CENTER
中環中心

**99 Queen's Rd Central, Central; admission free;** Ⓜ **Central (exit D)** 🚋

---

### BAD JOSS JOB

Many local people see the Bank of China Tower as a huge violation of the principles of feng shui. For example, the bank's four triangular prisms are negative symbols in the geomancer's rule book; being the opposite to circles, these contradict what circles suggest – perfection and (importantly in Hong Kong) prosperity. Furthermore, the huge crosses on the sides of the building suggest negativity and its shape has been likened to a praying mantis (a threatening symbol), complete with radio masts as antennae.

---

From close up, the protruding corners of this star-shaped, 73-storey building built in 1998 appear to cut into the structure. But what really sets it apart is the hypnotic nightly light show from almost 9000 neon tubes that send colour lights cascading down the towering 'spines' every 15 minutes.

## ◎ EXCHANGE SQUARE
交易廣場

**8 Connaught Place, Central; admission free;** Ⓜ **Central (exit A)** 🚋

This complex of three elevated office towers is home to the Hong Kong Stock Exchange and a number of businesses. Outside Towers I and II is a seating area surrounding a fountain, and several sculptures including one by Henry Moore. Below the square is Central bus station.

### ⊙ FORMER FRENCH MISSION BUILDING
前法國外方傳道會大樓

**1 Battery Path, Central; admission free;**
Ⓜ **Central (exit K)**

Just behind pretty Cheung Kong Park abutting St John's Cathedral is this charming structure built by an American trading firm in 1868. It served as the Russian Consulate in Hong Kong until 1915 when the French Overseas Mission bought it and added a chapel and a dome. Today it houses the Court of Final Appeal, the highest judicial body in Hong Kong.

### ⊙ GOVERNMENT HOUSE
香港禮賓府

☎ **2530 2003; Upper Albert Rd, Central; admission free;** Ⓨ **1 Sun in Mar;** 🚌 **3B, 12, 23, 103**

Parts of the one-time residence of Hong Kong's governors date back to 1853, though the commanding

---

**LIGHTING THE WAY**

Ice House St doglegs into Queen's Rd Central from the Dairy Farm Building, built in 1917 and now housing the Fringe Club (p71) and M at the Fringe (p65). Just before it turns north, a wide flight of stone steps leads down to Duddell St. The four wrought-iron China Gas lamps (Map p43, D3) at the top and bottom of the steps were placed here in the 1870s and are listed monuments.

---

tower was added by the Japanese during WWII. Both the current chief executive, Donald Tsang and his predecessor, Tung Chee Hwa, refused to take up residence here, ostensibly because the feng shui isn't quite right.

### ⊙ HONG KONG PLANNING & INFRASTRUCTURE EXHIBITION GALLERY
香港規劃及基建展覽館

☎ **3102 1242; www.gov.hk/infrastruc turegallery; 3 Edinburgh Pl, Central; admission free;** Ⓨ **10am-6pm Wed-Mon;** Ⓜ **Central (exit K)**

This gallery, with the mouthful of a name and next to the Low Block of Hong Kong City Hall (p55), takes visitors on a fascinating 18.5m 'walk' past recent, ongoing and future civil engineering, urban renewal and environment improvement projects in the territory.

### ⊙ HONG KONG ZOOLOGICAL & BOTANICAL GARDENS
香港動植物公園

☎ **2530 0154; www.lcsd.gov.hk/parks /hkzbg; Albany Rd, Central; admission free;** Ⓨ **terrace gardens 6am-10pm, zoo & aviaries 6am-7pm, greenhouses 9am-4.30pm;** 🚌 **3B, 12, 40, 40M**

These 5.6-hectare gardens, which first welcomed visitors in 1864, are a pleasant assembly of fountains, sculptures, greenhouses,

NEIGHBOURHOODS

CENTRAL & SHEUNG WAN

Burning incense at the Man Mo Temple

a playground, a zoo and some fab-ulous aviaries. There are hundreds of species of birds in residence as well as exotic trees, plants and

## NOT WALL FLOWERS

On Hong Kong Island only, and espe-cially in Central and Sheung Wan, you'll see what are called 'wall trees', ancient banyan trees (mostly) sprouting from openings in stone retaining walls. To prevent landslides on steep Hong Kong Island, masonry workers from the late 19th century until well after WWII shored up many slopes adjacent to main roads with retaining walls. Open joints between the stones allowed strong spe-cies such as Chinese banyans to sprout, further strengthening the walls. Today slopes are stabilised by cement.

shrubs. The zoo is surprisingly comprehensive and one of the world's leading centres for the captive breeding of endangered species. The gardens are divided by Albany Rd, with the plants and aviaries to the east off Garden Rd, and most of the animals to the west.

## ◙ HONGKONG & SHANGHAI BANK
香港上海匯豐銀行
**1 Queen's Rd Central, Central; admission free;** ☻ **9am-4.30pm Mon-Fri, 9am-12.30pm Sat;** Ⓜ **Central (exit K)** ☒
This 179m-tall glass-and-aluminium building is an innova-tive masterpiece. Locals call it the 'Robot Building' because you can see the chains and motors of the

escalators and other moving parts whirring away inside. Structurally, the building is equally as radical, built on a 'coat-hanger' frame, and remains the most expensive building ever erected.

### ⓒ JARDINE HOUSE
### 怡和大廈
**1 Connaught Pl, Central; admission free;** Ⓜ **Central (exit A)** 🚇
This 52-storey silver monolith was Hong Kong's first skyscraper when it opened as the Connaught Centre in 1973. The building's 1750 porthole-like windows have earned it a less respectable Chinese nickname: 'House of 1000 Arseholes'.

### ⓒ LEGISLATIVE COUNCIL BUILDING
### 立法會大樓
**8 Jackson Rd, Central; admission free;** Ⓜ **Central (exit J1)** 🚇
This colonnaded, domed neo-classical building is the former Supreme Court, built in 1912 of granite quarried on Stonecutter Island. Standing atop the pediment is a blindfolded statue of Themis, the Greek goddess of justice.

### ⓒ MAN MO TEMPLE
### 文武廟
☎ **2540 0350; 124-126 Hollywood Rd, Sheung Wan; admission free;** 🕐 **8am-6pm;** 🚌 **26**

The busy 'Civil and Martial' temple, one of the oldest in Hong Kong, is dedicated to a statesman of the 3rd century BC called Man Cheung, who is worshipped as the god of literature, and a military deity called Kwan Yu, a soldier born in the 2nd century AD and now venerated as the red-cheeked god of war.

### ⓒ PARA/SITE ART SPACE
### 藝術空間
☎ **2517 4620; www.para-site.org.hk; 4 Po Yan St, Sheung Wan; admission free;** 🕐 **noon-7pm Wed-Sun;** 🚌 **26**
This adventurous, artist-run space knows no boundaries when it

---

**DOWNSIZING & UPGRADING**

The IFC (International Finance Centre) Towers were partly designed by Cesar Pelli, the man responsible for Canary Wharf in London. One IFC, which opened in 1999, is a 'mere' 38 levels tall. At 88 storeys and almost 410m, Two IFC (p49), topped out in 2003, is currently Hong Kong's tallest building. But the International Commerce Center at Union Square (www.union-square.com.hk), a 118-storey, 484m development on reclaimed land above the Kowloon MTR and Airport Express station (which forms a 'gateway' for Victoria Harbour with Two IFC at the opposite side of the harbour) will claim the distinction in 2010.

comes to mixing media. Most art on display is local but there are occasional exhibitions by international artists as well.

### ⓒ ST JOHN'S CATHEDRAL
### 聖約翰座堂

☎ 2523 4157; www.stjohnscathedral .org.hk; 4-8 Garden Rd (enter from Battery Path), Central; admission free; ⏲ 7am-6pm; Ⓜ Central (exit J2)
Built in 1849, this Anglican cathedral, built in the shape of a cross, is one of the few colonial structures still standing in Central, and it's lost in a forest of skyscrapers. It suffered heavy damage during WWII; after the war the front

### SHEUNG WAN SHUFFLE

Sheung Wan is an excellent place to stroll around and can at times feel like stepping back in time. West of the Western Market (opposite) check out the dried seafood shops of Des Voeux Rd West, the herbal medicine wholesalers on Ko Shing St and the places selling bird's nests for soup and paper offerings for the dead on Queen's Rd West. Just opposite the Sheung Wan MTR station is Man Wa Lane, with stalls selling traditional carved chops (seals).

doors were remade using timber salvaged from the British warship, HMS *Tamar,* and the beautiful stained glass was replaced.

Hong Kong & Shanghai Bank headquarters (p46)

*We were wondering why there weren't any statues!*

## STATUE SQUARE
皇后像廣場 NOV 7/08

**Chater Rd & Des Voeux Rd Central, Central;** M **Central (exit K)**

This very central open space once displayed various effigies of British royalty, but these were carted away by the Japanese during WWII. The only statue that remains is the bronze of Sir Thomas Jackson, a particularly successful Victorian-era manager of the Hongkong & Shanghai Bank, which he now faces. On the northern side of Chater Rd is the Cenotaph (1923) dedicated to Hong Kong residents killed during the two world wars.

## TWO INTERNATIONAL FINANCE CENTRE
國際金融中心二期

☎ **2878 1111; wwwhkma.gov.hk; 8 Finance St, Central; admission free;** ⏰ **10am-6pm Mon-Fri, 10am-1pm Sat;** M **Hong Kong (exit F)**

At 88 storeys, Two IFC, sitting atop the terminus of the Airport Express and Tung Chung MTR lines, is Hong Kong's tallest building and has been christened 'Sir Y K Pao's Erection', a reference to the owner of the development company that built the tower. You can get as far as the 55th floor by visiting the **Hong Kong Monetary Authority Information Centre**, which contains exhibition areas related

to the Hong Kong currency, fiscal policy and banking history, and a research library. There are guided tours at 2.30pm Monday to Friday and at 10.30am on Saturday.

## WESTERN MARKET
西港城

**323 Des Voeux Rd Central & New Market St, Sheung Wan;** ⏰ **9am-7pm;** M **Sheung Wan (exit C)**

This three-storey Edwardian (1906) reopened in 1991 as a shopping centre to house textile vendors driven out of the lanes linking Queen's Rd and Des Voeux Rd Central. The ground floor has modern shops selling curios, jewellery and toys; the 1st floor has piece goods, with some decent silks.

---

### WORTH THE TRIP

East of Sheung Wan in Pok Fu Lam district is the **Hong Kong University Museum & Art Gallery** ( ☎ 2241 5500; www.hku.hk/hkumag; Fung Ping Shan Bldg, 94 Bonham Rd; admission free; ⏰ 9.30am-6pm Mon-Sat, 1.30-5.30pm Sun; 🚌 23, 40, 40M) containing important collections of ceramics and bronzes, plus a lesser number of paintings and carvings. There's an intriguing display of almost a thousand crosses made by Nestorians, a Christian sect that arose in Syria and moved into China during the 13th and 14th centuries.

---

NEIGHBOURHOODS

CENTRAL & SHEUNG WAN

# 🛍 SHOP

Central has a mix of midrange to top-end street-front retail and shopping malls; it's a good area to look for things like cameras, books, antiques and designer threads. Hollywood Rd, which links Central and Sheung Wan, is particularly good for antiques, fine art and curios while Stanley St in Central is one of the best spots for buying photographic equipment. For an 'only-in-Hong-Kong' experience, visit Li Yuen St East and West, two narrow alleyways that link Des Voeux Rd Central with Queen's Rd Central, and are a jumble of inexpensive clothing, handbags and jewellery.

## SUZIE WONG'S WARDROBE

Reach into any Hong Kong Chinese woman's closet and you're bound to find at least one cheongsam (*qipao* in Mandarin), the close-fitting sheath that is Hong Kong's national dress. It's worn on formal occasions such as Chinese New Year gatherings, to work (restaurant receptionists and nightclub hostesses wear them), to school (cotton cheongsams are still the uniform at several colleges and secondary schools) or for the 'big day'. Modern Hong Kong brides may take their vows in white, but before they slip off for the honeymoon, they put on a red cheongsam.

## 🛍 BLANC DE CHINE 源
*Clothing & Accessories*

☎ 2524 7875; Shop 201-203A, 2nd fl, Pedder Bldg, 12 Pedder St, Central; ⏰ 10am-7pm Mon-Sat, noon-5pm Sun; Ⓜ Central ♿

A sumptuous shop that specialises in men's traditional Chinese jackets, off the rack or made to measure, and women's silk dresses. There's also a an exquisite collection of satin bed linens.

## 🛍 DYMOCKS BOOKSELLERS 恬墨書舍 *Books*

☎ 2117 0360; www.dymocks.com .hk; Shop 2007-2011, 2nd fl, IFC Mall, 8 Finance St, Central; ⏰ 9.30am-9.30pm; Ⓜ Central, Hong Kong ♿

The large Australian chain offers a solid mainstream selection of page-turners, travel books, magazines and, in particular, books of local interest. This is one of its seven Hong Kong branches.

## 🛍 FOOK MING TONG TEA SHOP 福茗堂茶莊
*Food & Drink*

☎ 2295 0368; www.fookmingtong.com; Shop 3006, 3rd fl, IFC Mall, 8 Finance St, Central; ⏰ 10.30am-8pm Mon-Sat, 11am-8pm Sun; Ⓜ Central, Hong Kong ♿

Teas of various ages and propensities from gunpowder ($8 for 37.5g) to Nanyan Ti Guan Yin Crown Grade ($780 for 150g) and varied tea-making accoutrements.

## HANART TZ GALLERY
漢雅軒 *Fine Art*

☎ 2526 9019; www.hanart.com; Room 202, 2nd fl, Henley Bldg, 5 Queen's Rd Central, Central; ⏰ 10am-6.30pm Mon-Fri, 10am-6pm Sat; M Central (exit K) 🚇

One of the most influential and innovative galleries in Hong Kong, Hanart shows contemporary Chinese art with a thoroughbred stable of figurative and conceptual painters, sculptors and video artists, many of them based in Hong Kong.

## HONG KONG BOOK CENTRE *Books*

☎ 2522 7064; www.swindonbooks.com; basement, On Lok Yuen Bldg, 25 Des Voeux Rd Central; ⏰ 9am-6.30pm Mon-Fri, 9am-5.30pm Sat, 1-5pm Sun Jul & Aug; M Central (exit B) 🚇

This basement store has a vast selection of books and magazines, including a mammoth number of business titles.

## JOYCE
*Clothing & Accessories*

☎ 2810 1120; www.joyce.com; ground fl, New World Tower, 16 Queen's Rd Central; ⏰ 10.30am-7.30pm; M Central 🚇

Joyce Ma's multi-designer store (and Hong Kong institution) is a good choice if you're pressed for time, with Issey Miyake, Yves Saint Laurent, Comme des Garçons, Yohji Yamamoto and several Hong Kong designers on display.

---

### TRADITIONAL MEDICINE

The Chinese have been using traditional medicine for over three millennia and it's very popular in Hong Kong, both for prevention and cure. Mixtures might include fungi, buds, seeds and roots or even deer antlers or snake blood. The main regulatory body is the **Chinese Medicine Council of Hong Kong** ( ☎ 2121 1888; www.cmchk.org.hk).

---

## KING FOOK JEWELLERY
景福珠寶 *Jewellery*

☎ 2822 8573; www.kingfook.com; ground fl, King Fook Bldg, 30-32 Des Voeux Rd Central; ⏰ 9.30am-7pm; M Central 🚇

Established in 1949, King Fook, with its grandiose gilded entrance, stocks a large range of watches, top-end fountain pens and baubles.

## LIULIGONGFANG
琉璃工房 *Gifts & Souvenirs*

☎ 2973 0820; www.liuli.com; Shop 20-22, ground fl, Central Bldg, 1-3 Pedder St, Central; ⏰ 10am-7.30pm Mon-Sat, 10am-7pm Sun; M Central 🚇

A store with exquisite coloured objects, both practical (vases, candle holders) and ornamental (Buddhism figurines, jewellery) from a renowned Taiwan glass sculptress.

## 🏠 LOCK CHA TEA SHOP
樂茶軒 *Food & Drink*

☎ 2805 1360; upper ground fl, 290b Queen's Rd Central (enter from Ladder St), Sheung Wan; ⏱ 11am-7pm; Ⓜ Sheung Wan (exit A2)

This favourite shop sells Chinese teas, tea sets, wooden tea-boxes and well-presented gift packs of various cuppas. You can try before you buy.

## 🏠 SHANGHAI TANG
上海灘 *Clothing & Accessories*

☎ 2525 7333; www.shanghaitang.com; basement & ground fl, Pedder Bldg, 12 Pedder St, Central; ⏱ 10am-8pm Mon-Sat, noon-6pm Sun; Ⓜ Central 🅿

This stylish shop has sparked something of a fashion wave with its updated versions of traditional yet neon-coloured Chinese garments. Shanghai Tang also has accessories and delightful gift items on sale.

## 🏠 TOY MUSEUM *Toys*

☎ 2869 9138; Shop 320, 3rd fl, Prince's Bldg, 10 Chater Rd, Central; ⏱ 10am-7pm Mon-Sat, noon-5.30pm Sun; Ⓜ Central 🅿

Top-of-the-line teddy bears, beanie babies and Pokemon paraphernalia are on sale at this cluttered shop. There's a great collection of old GI Joes and other action men for dads to amuse themselves with.

# 🍴 EAT

## 🍴 CITY HALL MAXIM'S PALACE 大會堂美心皇宮
*Dim sum* $$

☎ 2521 1303; 3rd fl, Low Block, Hong Kong City Hall, 1 Edinburgh Pl, Central; ⏱ 11am-3pm & 5.30-11.30pm Mon-Sat, 9am-11.30pm Sun; Ⓜ Central

If you want to experience real, live Hong Kong dim sum, with all its clatter and clutter, head for this place in Hong Kong City Hallo on Saturday or Sunday morning. Cacophonous but delectable!

## 🍴 CITY'SUPER *Supermarket*

☎ 2234 7128; www.citysuper.com.hk; Shop 1041-1049, 1st fl, IFC Mall, 8 Finance St, Central; ⏱ 10.30am-10pm; Ⓜ Central 🅿

Gourmet supermarket with ready-to-eats such as sushi and salads, and fresh produce that has been flown in at relatively high prices.

## 🍴 HUNAN GARDEN
洞庭樓 *Hunanese* $$$

☎ 2868 2880; 3rd fl, The Forum, Exchange Square, Connaught Rd Central, Central; ⏱ 11.30am-3pm & 5.30-11.30pm; Ⓜ Central

This elegant place specialises in spicy Hunanese cuisine, which is often hotter that the Sichuanese variety. The Hunanese fried chicken with chilli is excellent, as are the seafood dishes.

## Michaelle Garnaut,
*Owner of M at the Fringe (p65)*

**The beginning:** I got a job as one of the first female cooks here. 'Why do you want to cook?' they all asked me. 'You'll make more money waiting tables.' **Western food then?** Swiss-German chefs ran most of the restaurants so it was heavy, very continental. Or it was British colonial – fish and chips and the like. **And today?** Most of the restaurants are controlled by seven or eight groups so creativity is diluted. It's not a very interesting dining scene at the moment. **Chinese food?** I like the communality of Chinese food, the sharing, the round tables. **Can't wait to get back to:** The landscape and the order, compared with Shanghai. **Hong Kong in a word or two:** Hong Kong is a psychotic city that doesn't know what it is. For that reason, everyone can find a place in it. **Perfect day out:** A walk in the hills, a browse in the flower market, a bowl of won ton soup.

NEIGHBOURHOODS

CENTRAL & SHEUNG WAN

Open-air diners, Central

## 🍴 KATONG 加東

*Singaporean* $

☎ 2543 4008; 8 Mercer St, Sheung Wan;
⏲ 11.30am-9pm Mon-Sat, 11.30am-
8pm Sun; Ⓜ Sheung Wan

Down a narrow street in Sheung
Wan is this new little Singaporean eatery serving some of the
best (and most authentic) laksa
(prawns and noodles cooked in
a coconut broth) this side of the
causeway.

## 🍴 KOREA HOUSE 梨花園

*Korean* $$

☎ 2544 0007; ground fl, Honwell
Commercial Centre, 119-121 Connaught
Rd Central, Sheung Wan (enter from Man
Wa Lane); ⏲ noon-11pm; Ⓜ Sheung
Wan

This comfortable restaurant serves
a delicious array of appetisers
(dried fish, pickles, *kimchi*) as side
dishes to the barbecue sizzling at
your table.

## ⊞ LEUNG HING RESTAURANT
兩興潮州海鮮飯店

*Chiu Chow*  $$

☎ 2850 6666; 32 Bonham Strand West, Sheung Wan; ⏱ 11am-11pm; Ⓜ Sheung Wan

The staple ingredients of Chiu Chow cuisine (shellfish, goose and duck) are extensively employed and delectably prepared at this very local place. Bring a native speaker or use your hands.

## ⊞ TSUI WAH 翠華餐廳
*Cantonese* Nov 8/08  $

☎ 2525 6338; ground, 1st & 2nd fl, 15-19 Wellington St, Central; ⏱ 6.30am-4am; Ⓜ Central

Anyone who spends any length of time in Hong Kong ends up slurping noodles at the territory's favourite late-night eatery at least once. Added bonus: it's something of a pulling place for every persuasion. *Hong Kong style café - noodles were good (went out at lunch)*

## 🍸 DRINK

## 🍸 CAPTAIN'S BAR *Bar* but not of and.

☎ 2522 0111; ground fl, Mandarin Oriental, 5 Connaught Rd Central, Central; ⏱ 11am-2am Mon-Sat, 11am-1am Sun; Ⓜ Central

This clubby, suited place remains just as comfortable and familiar as it did before the Mandarin Oriental got a massive face-lift. It serves ice-cold draught beer in chilled silver mugs and some of the best martinis in town, and is a good place to talk business. It's also set up for play with it's mini dance-floor.

## ⭐ PLAY

## ⭐ HONG KONG CITY HALL
香港大會堂

*Live Music, Dance, Theatre*

☎ 2921 2840, bookings 2734 9009; www.cityhall.gov.hk; Low Block, 1 Edinburgh Pl, Central; tickets $80-750; Ⓜ Central

Built in 1962, Hong Kong City Hall is still a major cultural venue in Hong Kong, with concert and recital halls, a theatre and exhibition galleries.

## ⭐ PALACE IFC CINEMA
*Cinema*

☎ 2388 6268; Podium L1, IFC Mall, 8 Finance St, Central; tickets $40-70; ⏱ 11.30am-midnight Mon-Fri, 9.30am-1am Sat, 9.30am-midnight Sun; Ⓜ Central, Hong Kong

This five-screen cinema complex is the most advanced and comfortable cinematic experience in the territory.

# >HONG KONG ISLAND: LAN KWAI FONG & SOHO

Lan Kwai Fong and Soho, actually divisions of Central, are relatively new but integral neighbourhoods that have helped pulled the crowds back to this part of Hong Kong Island. Much of Central's nightlife revolves around Lan Kwai Fong, a narrow alleyway that doglegs south and then west from D'Aguilar St. In the not-so-distant past it was an area of squalid

## LAN KWAI FONG & SOHO

### ◉ SEE
Central Escalator ............ 1 B3

### 🏠 SHOP
Amours Antiques .......... 2 A3
Arch Angel Antiques ..... 3 B3
Arch Angel
Contemporary Art ......... 4 B3
Caravan ........................ 5 B2
Chine Gallery ................ 6 B3
Dialogue ....................... 7 A3
Eu Yan Sang .................. 8 C2
Flow Organic Bookshop.. 9 C3
Grotto Fine Art ........... 10 C5
Hing Lee Camera
Company ..................... 11 B3
Hobbs & Bishops Fine
Art .............................. 12 B3
Karin Weber Antiques .. 13 B2
Linva Tailor ................. 14 C3
Mir Oriental Carpets.... 15 C5
Mountain Folkcraft ..... 16 D4
Photo Scientific........... 17 D4
Plum Blossoms ............ 18 C3
Rock Candy .................. 19 B2
Spy Soho...................... 20 B3
Tai Yip Art Book Centre.. 21 C3
Tibetan Gallery............ 22 C4
Wah Tung Ceramic Arts.. 23 B3
Wattis Fine Art ............ 24 B3

### 🍴 EAT
2 Sardines.................... 25 B4
Beirut ......................... 26 D4
Bombay Dreams........... 27 C3
Chedi .......................... 28 B4
Chez Patrick................ 29 B3
Da Ping Huo................ 30 B3
Finds .......................... 31 C5
Flying Pan .................. 32 B4
Good Luck Thai Food.... 33 C4
Graham St Market ....... 34 B2
Life ............................. 35 B3
Lin Heung Tea House.... 36 B2
Luk Yu Tea House ........ 37 D3
M at the Fringe        (see 66)
Nha Trang ................... 38 C3
Rughetta..................... 39 C3
Shui Hu Ju ................. 40 A3
Tsui Wah .................... 41 D4
Yi Jiang Nan ............... 42 B3
Yung Kee ..................... 43 D4

### 🍸 DRINK
Bacar .......................... 44 B3
Bar 1911 ..................... 45 B3
Barco .......................... 46 A3
Bit Point ..................... 47 C4
Club 71 ....................... 48 B2
Club Feather Boa ......... 49 A3

Dragon 1 ..................... 50 C4
Gecko Lounge.............. 51 C3
Havana ....................... 52 A4
Joyce is Not Here ........ 53 B3
Nzingha Longe ............ 54 B3
Peak Cafe Bar ............. 55 B4
Soda ........................... 56 C3
Staunton's Wine Bar &
Cafe ............................ 57 B4

### ⭐ PLAY
Bliss                        (see 19)
Blue Door.................... 58 C3
Bohemian Lounge........ 59 B3
C Club ........................ 60 D4
California Fitness ........ 61 D4
Cavern ........................ 62 C4
Club 97 ....................... 63 D4
DK Aromatherapy......... 64 B3
Drop............................ 65 B3
Fringe Club, Theatre &
Studio......................... 66 D5
Happy Foot
Reflexology................. 67 C3
Home........................... 68 C3
Propaganda................. 69 C3
Pure Fitness ............... 70 B3
Sense of Touch ........... 71 C5
Works ......................... 72 C5
Yoga Fitness ............... 73 D5
Yumla                       (see 56)

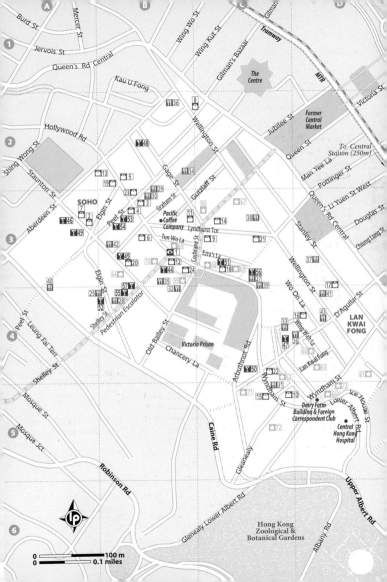

tenements, rubbish and rats, but it has since been scrubbed, face-lifted and closed to traffic. Lan Kwai Fong's clientele tends to be relatively young and upwardly mobile, and expats mix easily with local business types and trendies. It's without a doubt the best and most complete bar strip in the territory. Nearby Soho (short for 'south of Hollywood Rd') is more geared for dining than drinking, but there are a couple of bars and clubs worth the trek – on foot or via the Central Escalator – up the hill. In fact, there is nothing but eateries (of varying quality) lining Elgin St.

# 👁 SEE

## 🇨 CENTRAL ESCALATOR
中環至半山自動扶梯

☎ 2523 7488; Cochrane, Shelley & Peel Sts, Central; admission free; 🕑 down 6-10am, up 10.20am-midnight; Ⓜ Central (exit C) 🚌

The world's longest covered outdoor people-mover is part commuter travolator, part sightseeing ride and part pick-up procession. It consists of elevated escalators, moving walkways and linking stairs on the 800m hill from Central's offices to the bedroom communities of the Mid-Levels. The best part is gliding by the Shelley St bars; there's just enough time to make flirtatious eye contact with the denizens within.

# 🛍 SHOP

## 🇨 AMOURS ANTIQUES
*Antiques, Clothing & Accessories*

☎ 2803 7877; 45 Staunton St, Soho; 🕑 noon-9pm Mon-Sat, noon-7pm Sun; 🚌 26

This wonderful shop stocks rhinestone jewellery, frocks and a darling clutch of beaded and tapestry bags dating from the early 20th century.

## 🇨 ARCH ANGEL ANTIQUES
*Antiques, Fine Art*

☎ 2851 6848; www.archangelgalleries .com; 53-55 Hollywood Rd, Central; 🕑 9.30am-6.30pm; 🚌 26

Though its specialities are ancient porcelain and tomb ware, Arch Angel packs a lot more into its three floors: everything from mah-jong sets and terracotta horses to palatial furniture. It also runs an art gallery, **Arch Angel Contemporary Art** ( ☎ 2851 6882; 58 Hollywood Rd, Central; 🕑 9.30am-6.30pm), which is across the road and deals in fine art.

## 🇨 CARAVAN *Carpets*

☎ 2547 3821; 65 Hollywood Rd, Central; 🕑 10.30am-6.30pm; 🚌 26

A shop called Caravan with an owner named Driver? Trustworthy rug-sellers travel all over Asia to stock this nicely cluttered shop.

The range of Afghan and Tibetan carpets is especially notable.

### 🏠 CHINE GALLERY
華 *Antiques*

☎ 2543 0023; www.chinegallery.com; 42a Hollywood Rd, Soho; ⏰ 10am-6pm Mon-Sat, 1-6pm Sun; 🚌 13, 26, 40M
This delightful shop sells carefully restored furniture (we love the lacquered cabinets) from all over China and hand-knotted rugs from remote regions such as Xinjiang, Ningxia, Gansu, Inner Mongolia and Tibet.

### 🏠 EU YAN SANG
余仁生 *Medicine*

☎ 2544 3870; www.euyansang.com; 152-156 Queen's Rd Central, Soho; ⏰ 9am-7.30pm; Ⓜ Central
Eu Yan Sang, with branches throughout Hong Kong, is the town's most famous dispenser of traditional Chinese medicines, and the staff speak good English. It's also an interesting place to browse as many of the healing ingredients are displayed and explained.

### 🏠 FLOW ORGANIC BOOKSHOP
流動的心情書店 *Books*

☎ 2964 9483; 1st & 2nd fl, Lyndhurst Tce (enter from Cochrane St), Central; ⏰ noon-7.30pm; 🚌 13, 26
We're not entirely sure what makes this secondhand and

exchange bookstore 'organic' but it does have something of a focus on spiritual and New Age literature.

### 🏠 GROTTO FINE ART
嘉圖現代藝術有限公司 *Fine Art*

☎ 2121 2270; www.grottofineart .com; 2nd fl, 31C-D Wyndham St, Central; ⏰ 11am-7pm Mon-Sat
This small but exquisite gallery represents predominantly Hong Kong artists whose work covers everything from painting and sculpture to mixed media.

### 🏠 HING LEE CAMERA COMPANY 興利相機公司
*Photographic Equipment*

☎ 2544 7593; 25 Lyndhurst Tce, Central; ⏰ 9.30am-7pm Mon-Sat, 11am-5pm Sun; Ⓜ Central 🚌 13, 40M
A reputable outlet with new and secondhand 35mm camera bodies and lenses, as well as midrange compact and digital cameras.

### 🏠 HOBBS & BISHOPS FINE ART 藝之 *Antiques*

☎ 2537 9838; 28 Hollywood Rd, Soho; ⏰ 10am-5.30pm Mon-Sat; 🚌 13, 26, 40M
This shop smells of beeswax and specialises in lacquered Chinese wooden furniture from the 19th and early 20th centuries. The buyer's taste leans toward the sleekly handsome rather than the glitzy.

Arch Angel Antiques (p58)

 **KARIN WEBER ANTIQUES**
*Antiques & Fine Art*
☎ 2544 5004; www.karinwebergallery
.com; 20 Aberdeen St, Soho; ⏱ 11am-
7pm Mon-Sat; 🚌 26
Karin Weber has a good mix of
Chinese country antiques and contemporary Asian artworks. She gives
short and useful lectures on antiques and the scene in Hong Kong.

🏠 **LINVA TAILOR**
年華時裝公司 *Clothing &
Accessories*
☎ 2544 2456; 38 Cochrane St, Central;
⏱ 9.30am-6.30pm Mon-Sat; 🚌 13, 40M

This is the place to come to buy or
have your own cheongsam (p50)
stitched up. Bring your own silk or
choose from Mr Leung's selection.

🏠 **MOUNTAIN FOLKCRAFT**
高山民藝 *Gifts & Souvenirs*
☎ 2523 2817; 12 Wo On Lane, Central;
⏱ 9.30am-6.30pm Mon-Sat; Ⓜ Central
One of the nicest shops in town
for folk crafts. There's batik, clothing, woodcarvings and lacquer-
ware made by Chinese and other
Asian ethnic minorities. Shop
attendants are friendly, and prices
reasonable.

## 🎁 MIR ORIENTAL CARPETS
*Carpets*

☎ 2521 5641; ground fl, New India House, 52 Wyndham St, Central; ⌚ 10am-6.30pm Mon-Sat, 11am-5pm Sun; 🚌 13, 26, 40M

One of Hong Kong's largest stockists of fine rugs, with thousands of carpets from around the world flying in and out of its shop. It is Hong Kong's top specialist for Persian carpets, both traditional and modern.

## 🎁 PHOTO SCIENTIFIC
攝影科學 *Photographic Equipment*

☎ 2525 0550; ground fl, Eurasia Bldg, 6 Stanley St, Central; ⌚ 9am-7pm Mon-Sat; Ⓜ Central

This shop is the favourite of Hong Kong's professional photographers. You may find cheaper equipment elsewhere, but Photo Scientific has a rock-solid reputation, with labelled prices and no bargaining.

## 🎁 PLUM BLOSSOMS
萬玉堂 *Fine Art*

☎ 2521 2189; www.plumblossoms.com; ground fl, Chinachem Hollywood Centre, 1 Hollywood Rd, Central; ⌚ 10am-6.30pm Mon-Sat; Ⓜ Central (exit D2) 🚌 26

The gallery where the late Rudolf Nureyev used to buy his baubles (and other celebrities continue to do so) is one of the most interesting and well established in Hong Kong.

## 🎁 ROCK CANDY *Jewellery*

☎ 2549 1018 www.rockcandy.hk 1 Elgin St, Soho; ⌚ 11am-8pm Mon-Sat; 🚌 26

Made from black glass and with pin-prick lights illuminating display cases, this goth-glam jewellery shop (and its ubertrendy gewgaws) has to be seen to be believed.

## 🎁 TAI YIP ART BOOK CENTRE
大業 *Books*

☎ 2524 5963; www.taiyipart.com.hk; Room 101-102, 1st fl, Capitol Plaza, 2-10 Lyndhurst Tce, Central; ⌚ 10am-7pm Mon-Fri, 10am-6.30pm Sat & Sun; Ⓜ Central

Tai Yip has a terrific selection of books about anything that is Chinese and arty: calligraphy, jade, bronze, costumes, architecture, symbolism. There are outlets in several of Hong Kong's museums including the Hong Kong Museum of Art (p112).

## 🎁 TIBETAN GALLERY
西藏古董藝廊 *Antiques*

☎ 2530 4863; ground & 1st fl, 55 Wyndham St, Central; ⌚ 10.30am-7pm Mon-Sat; 🚌 13, 26, 40M

This small shop has an impressive selection of Tibetan religious art and artefacts, including mini-altars. It also houses a vast array of antique Tibetan rugs. There's a showroom on the 1st floor.

## 🎁 WAH TUNG CERAMIC ARTS 華通陶瓷
*Gifts & Souvenirs*

☎ 2543 2823; www.wahtungchina.com; 59 Hollywood Rd, Central; 🕙 10am-7pm; 🚌 26

The world's largest supplier of hand-decorated ceramics, Wah Tung has everything from brightly painted vases and ginger jars to reproduction Tang dynasty figurines. And what you don't see, they'll source for you.

## 🎁 WATTIS FINE ART *Antiques*

☎ 2524 5302; www.wattis.com.hk; 2nd fl, 20 Hollywood Rd, Soho; 🕙 10am-6pm Tue-Sat, 1-5pm Sun; 🚌 26

No place in Hong Kong has a better collection of antique maps for sale than this place; the selection of old photographs of Hong Kong and Macau is also very impressive. Enter from Old Bailey St.

# 🍴 EAT

## 🍴 2 SARDINES
*French*                                    $$$

☎ 2973 6618; 43 Elgin St, Soho; 🕙 noon-2.30pm & 6-10.30pm; 🚌 13, 12, 26

This independent French bistro, almost an old-timer on the transient Soho restaurant scene, deserves the crowds it draws. The namesake fish (grilled) and the roast rack of lamb are among the hearty and homey dishes worth trying. The wine list leans predictably to the Gallic side and is well chosen.

## 🍴 BEIRUT *Lebanese*                     $$$

☎ 2804 6611; Shop A, Winner Bldg, 27-39 D'Aguilar St, Lan Kwai Fong; 🕙 noon-3pm & 6-11.30pm Mon-Sat, 6-11pm Sun; Ⓜ Central

This affable, slightly cramped Lebanese restaurant has a long bar that looks out onto Lan Kwai Fong. It serves authentic Lebanese dishes such as *kibbeh* (spicy meatballs) and *lahme bil agine* ('pizza' with minced lamb).

## 🍴 BOMBAY DREAMS *Indian*               $$

☎ 2971 0001; 1st fl, Carfield Commercial Bldg, 75-77 Wyndham St, Central; 🕙 noon-3.30pm & 6-11pm; Ⓜ Central

This curry house is convenient to the pubs of Lan Kwai Fong and serves relatively authentic Indian fare in upmarket surrounds.

## 🍴 CHEDI *Thai*                          $

☎ 2868 4445; 38 Elgin St, Soho; 🕙 noon-11pm; 🚌 26

This attractive restaurant, with warm backlit walls and tiny courtyard, serves some of the most authentic Thai food in upbeat, stylish surrounds. There are heaps of choices for vegetarians and – unusual for a Southeast Asian restaurant – the wine list is excellent.

## BEST FOOT & FACE FORWARD

Dining in Hong Kong is an all-in affair: everyone shares dishes, chats loudly and makes a mess. Food is to be enjoyed whole-heartedly, not picked at discreetly. There are, however, a few points of etiquette it doesn't hurt to know about.

> Wait for others to start before digging in (though as a guest you may be encouraged to start).
> Say thank you if someone puts food into your bowl – this is a courteous gesture.
> Cover your mouth with your hand when using a toothpick.
> Don't try to clean up dishes and detritus – a stained tablecloth is a sign of a good meal.
> Don't be afraid to ask for a fork if you can't manage chopsticks (most Chinese restaurants have them).
> Don't stick chopsticks upright into rice as they can look like incense sticks in a bowl of ashes – a sign of death.
> Don't flip a fish over to reach the flesh on the bottom as the next fishing boat you pass will capsize.

### 🍴 CHEZ PATRICK *French* $$$$

☎ 2541 1401; 26 Peel St, Central; ⏱ noon-3pm & 6.30-10.30pm; Ⓜ Central

This very stylish and very French new *gosse* (that's 'kid' *en français*) on the block is a welcome addition to Central's menu, where authenticity often proves elusive. It has restful black-and-white décor, and the set lunches are excellent value.

### 🍴 DA PING HUO
大平伙 *Sichuanese* $$

☎ 2559 1317, 9051 4496; lower ground fl, 49 Hollywood Rd, Central; ⏱ 6pm-midnight; 🚌 26

This very stylish, minimalist eatery below Hollywood Rd serves fiery Sichuanese set meals, at the end of which the owner-chef emerges to sing Chinese opera. Be sure to book ahead.

### 🍴 FINDS *Scandinavian* $$$$

☎ 2522 9318; 2nd fl, Lan Kwai Fong Tower, 33 Wyndham St, Central; ⏱ noon-2.30pm & 7-11pm; 🚌 13, 26, 40M

This wonderful place, whose name is an acronym for all the Nordic countries, serves light and very tasty Scandinavian food. The surrounds – faux igloo walls, icicle-dripping chandelier, lots of blue tones – is a cool oasis. There's a gay happy hour called Ice on the first Wednesday of each month (6.30pm to 9pm).

### 🍴 FLYING PAN *Café & Deli* $

☎ 2140 6333; 9 Old Bailey St, Soho; ⏱ 24hr; 🚌 13, 26, 40M

This place with the silly name takes its breakfasts very seriously and around the clock. Stumble here from the pubs and clubs of

Vendor at Graham St Market

the Fong and tuck into anything from an omelette to a full fry-up.

### 🍴 GOOD LUCK THAI FOOD
好運泰國菜 *Thai*                    $
☎ 2877 2971; 13 Wing Wah Lane, Lan Kwai Fong; ⏱ 11am-2am Mon-Sat, 4pm-midnight Sun; Ⓜ Central
After sinking a few beers in Lan Kwai Fong, make your way over to this chaotic but friendly place at the slops end of the charmingly nicknamed 'Rat Alley' for a cheap fix of late-night Thai food.

### 🍴 GRAHAM ST MARKET
歌賦街市場 *Market*
Graham St, Soho; ⏱ 6am-8pm; Ⓜ Central

The stalls and shops lining Graham St south of (and up the hill from) Queen's Rd Central to Hollywood Rd are positively groaning with high-quality vegetables and fruit, as well as meat, seafood and other comestibles. If you don't visit any other Hong Kong 'wet market', come to this one for thrills, chills and no doubt spills.

### 🍴 LIFE *Vegetarian*              $
☎ 2810 9777; 10 Shelly St, Soho; ⏱ noon-midnight Mon-Fri, 10am-midnight Sat & Sun; 🚌 26
Life is a vegetarian's dream come true, serving vegan food and dishes free of gluten, wheat, onion and garlic. There's a delicatessen

---

**BOOKING & TIPPING**

It's advisable to book ahead in all but the cheapest restaurants, especially on Friday and Saturday night. Most restaurants add a 10% service charge to the bill. If the service at a top-end restaurant was outstanding, you might consider adding another 5% or 10% on top of the service charge. At cheap or midrange places, a couple of coins is sufficient.

---

and shop (8am to 10.30pm weekdays, 9am to 10.30pm Saturday and Sunday) on the ground floor, a café on the first and seating on the rooftop garden.

### 🍴 LIN HEUNG TEA HOUSE
蓮香樓 *Cantonese*                    $

☎ 2544 4556; 160-164 Wellington St, Central; 🕑 6am-11pm; Ⓜ Central
This older-style Cantonese restaurant is worth a visit for the tableau: old men reading the newspaper, extended families chatting and large office groups noshing. There's decent dim sum served from trolleys so it's good for a late bite or those eating alone.

### 🍴 LUK YU TEA HOUSE
陸羽茶室 *Dim Sum*                   $$

☎ 2523 5464; 24-26 Stanley St, Central; 🕑 7am-10pm; Ⓜ Central
This old-style teahouse is a museum piece in more ways than one. Most of the staff have been

here since the early Ming dynasty and are as grumpy as an emperor deposed. Still it's *the* place for tasty dim sum (7am to 5pm) in atmospheric surrounds.

### 🍴 M AT THE FRINGE
*International*                      $$$$

☎ 2877 4000; 1st fl, Fringe Club, Dairy Farm Bldg, 2 Lower Albert Rd, Central; 🕑 noon-2.30pm Mon-Fri, 7-10.30pm daily; Ⓜ Central
No-one seems to have a bad thing to say about Michelle's. The menu changes constantly, and everything is consistently excellent, be it crab soufflé, the foie gras two ways or the famous slow-baked salted lamb. It's worth saving room for the splendid desserts.

### 🍴 NHA TRANG
芽莊 *Vietnamese*                    $

☎ 2581 9992 88 Wellington St, Central; 🕑 noon-11pm; Ⓜ Central
The regular Vietnamese clientele at this simple but stylish restaurant is testament to the quality and authenticity of the food.

### 🍴 RUGHETA *Italian*              $$$

☎ 2537 7922; basement, Carfield Commercial Bldg, 75-77 Wyndham St, Central; 🕑 11.30am-2.30pm Mon-Sat, 6.30-10.30pm Sun-Thu, 6.30-11pm Fri & Sat; Ⓜ Central
This basement restaurant, which has a branch in New York City,

serves faultless 'Roman' (read earthy Italian) cuisine – though avoid it at lunchtime when the masses descend (literally).

### 🍴 SHUI HU JU 水滸居
*Sichuanese* $$

☎ 2869 6927; 68 Peel St, Soho; 🕐 6pm–midnight; 🚌 26
This restaurant serves earthy, chilli-packed Sichuanese dishes (at dinner only) in a delightful Chinese setting that feels like you're dining in one of the neighbouring antiques shops.

### 🍴 YI JIANG NAN
憶江南 *Shanghainese & Northern Chinese* $$

☎ 2136 0886; 33-35 Staunton St, Soho; 🕐 noon-3pm & 6-11pm; Ⓜ Central
This place has excellent (and quite enlightened) Shanghainese and Northern Chinese cuisine. Meals are served on black wooden tables under birdcages moonlighting as lanterns and rather fetching murals.

### 🍴 YUNG KEE
鏞記酒家 *Cantonese* $$$

☎ 2522 1624; 32-40 Wellington St, Central; 🕐 11am-11.30pm; Ⓜ Central (exit D2)
This long-standing institution is probably the most famous Cantonese restaurant in Hong Kong. Yung Kee's roast goose has been the talk of the town since

---

### HAPPY HOUR
During certain hours of the day, most pubs, bars and even some clubs give discounts on drinks (usually one-third to one-half off) or offer a two-for-one deal. Happy hour is usually in the late afternoon or early evening (eg 4pm to 8pm) but the times vary widely from place to place. Depending on the season, the day of the week and the location, some pub happy hours run from midday till as late as 10pm, and some resume after midnight for an hour or so.

---

1942, and its dim sum (2pm to 5.30pm Monday to Saturday, 11am to 5.30pm Sunday) is excellent.

## 🍸 DRINK

### 🍸 BACAR *Wine Bar*
☎ 2521 8325; 22 Shelley St, Soho; 🕐 10am-2am; 🚌 13, 26, 40M
This intimate wine brasserie (whose name means 'Wine Goblet' in Latin, apparently) is the place to go if your palate leans toward the bacchanalia of the grape rather than hops. The selection of wines is impressive and a couple of tables at the front are top-notch spots for a bit of Central Escalator cruising.

### 🍸 BAR 1911 *Bar*
☎ 2810 6681; 7 Staunton St, Soho; 🕐 5pm-midnight Mon-Sat, happy hour 5-9pm; Ⓜ Central

This is a very refined bar with fine details (stained glass, ceiling fans, lanterns) and a 1920s vibe.

### Y BARCO *Wine Bar*
☎ 2857 4478; 42 Staunton St, Soho; 🕑 4pm-1am Sun-Thu, 4pm-late Fri & Sat, happy hour 4-8pm; Ⓜ Central
One of our favourite Soho bars, Barco has great staff, is small enough to never feel empty and attracts a cool mix of locals and expats.

### Y BIT POINT *Pub*
☎ 2523 7436; 31 D'Aguilar St, Lan Kwai Fong; 🕑 noon-3am Mon-Fri, noon-4am Sat, 4pm-1am Sun, happy hour 3-9pm; Ⓜ Central
Owned by the same lot as Biergarten, Bit Point is essentially a German-style bar, where beer drinking is taken very seriously indeed. Most beers here are draught pilsners and there's some solid Teutonic fare on offer as blotter.

### Y CLUB 71 *Bar*
☎ 2858 7071; basement, 67 Hollywood Rd, Central; 🕑 3pm-2am Mon-Sat, 6pm-1am Sun, happy hour 3-9pm; 🚌 26
When Club 64, the counter-culture nerve centre of Lan Kwai Fong (a name recalling the 4 June 1989 Tiananmen Square massacre in Beijing) was forced to close, some of the owners relocated to this alley north of Hollywood Rd. Named after the huge protest march held

on 1 July 2003, Club 71 is again one of the best drinking spots for nonposers. Get to it via a small footpath running west off Peel St.

### Y CLUB FEATHER BOA *Bar*
☎ 2857 2586; 38 Staunton St, Soho; 🕑 8pm-late Tue-Sat; Ⓜ Central
Feather Boa is a plush lounge hidden behind gold drapes. Part camp lounge, part bordello – part those curtains and get stuck into one of their infamous mango daiquiris.

### Y DRAGON-I *Bar*
☎ 3110 1222; upper ground fl, The Centrium, 60 Wyndham St, Central; 🕑 noon-midnight Mon-Sat, happy hour 5-9pm; Ⓜ Central
This delightful venue on the edge of Soho has both an indoor bar and restaurant and a huge terrace over Wyndham St filled with caged songbirds. You'd *almost* think you were in the country.

### Y GECKO LOUNGE *Live-Music Bar*
☎ 2537 4680; lower ground fl, 15-19 Hollywood Rd, Central (enter from Ezra's Lane off Cochrane St or Pottinger St); 🕑 4pm-3am Mon-Thu, 4pm-6am Fri & Sat, happy hour 6-9pm; Ⓜ Central
Gecko is a relaxed hide-out that attracts a fun crowd, especially to its live jazz sessions Tuesday to Thursday. The well-hidden DJ mixes good grooves with kooky

Parisian tunes at the weekend. There's a great wine list.

### ☂ HAVANA *Bar*

☎ 2545 9966; 35 Elgin St, Soho; ⏱ 11am-midnight; 🚌 13, 12, 26
Some people come to this Elgin St stalwart for the Cuban combination platters (including a yummy vegetarian option) and to watch the world go by on the tiny terrace. We recommend the latter, but with one of Hong Kong's best mojitos in hand.

### ☂ NZINGHA LOUNGE *Bar*

☎ 2834 6366; basement, Garley Bldg, 48-52A Peel St, Soho; ⏱ noon-late Mon-Sat, happy hour 5-9pm; Ⓜ Central
This African bar and restaurant has regular events and is also just a cool place in which to chill out. It's nonsmoking – unusual for Hong Kong.

### ☂ PEAK CAFE BAR
山頂餐廳 *Bar & Café*

☎ 2140 6877; 9-13 Shelley St, Soho; ⏱ 11am-2am Mon-Sat, 11am-midnight Sun, happy hour 5-8pm; 🚌 13, 26, 40M
The fixtures and fittings of the much-missed Peak Cafe, from 1947, have moved down the hill to this comfy bar with super cocktails and excellent nosh. The only thing missing is the view.

### ☂ SODA *Bar*

☎ 2522 8118; upper basement, 79 Wyndham St, Central (enter from Pottinger St); ⏱ 4pm-midnight Sun-Thu, 4pm-3am Fri & Sat, happy hour 6-9pm; 🚌 13, 26, 40M
This well-placed watering hole, decorated in warm yellows and oranges, and with its front open to steep Pottinger St, is also a DJ scene, notably on Wednesday and the weekend, with hip-hop and R & B.

## WHAT'S ON WHERE & WHEN

**Artslink** A monthly with listings of performances, exhibitions and art-house film screenings. Published by the Hong Kong Arts Centre (www.hkac.org.hk).

**Cityline** ( ☎ 2314 4228; www.cityline.com.hk) Affiliate of Urbtix; also good for bookings.

**bc magazine** (www.bcmagazine.net) A free biweekly guide to Hong Kong's entertainment and partying scene.

**HK Magazine** (www.asia-city.com) A very comprehensive entertainment listings magazine. It's free, appears on Friday and can be found at restaurants, bars, shops and hotels.

**hkclubbing.com** (www.hkclubbing.com) Especially useful for clubbing and parties.

**Urbtix** ( ☎ 2111 5999; www.urbtix.gov.hk) Bookings for most cultural events can be made online or by phone.

Staunton's Wine Bar & Cafe

## ★ PLAY

### ☆ BLISS Club
☎ 3110 1222, 2147 2122; basement & ground fl, 1 Elgin St, Soho; ☉ 5.30pm-late Mon-Sat, 2-11pm Sun, happy hour 6-9pm; 🚌 26

What was a popular postwork suit hang-out called Liquid then a sophisticated lounge-cum-dance-bar called NU has metamorphosed into Hong Kong's newest low-key gay club, with a basement, two bars and ultrasophisticated lounge. You can't miss the joint; it's next to eye-popping Rock Candy (p61).

### ☆ BLUE DOOR Live Music
☎ 2858 6555; www.bluedoor.com.hk; 5th fl, Cheung Hing Commercial Bldg, 37 Cochrane St, Central (enter from Gage St), Central; ☉ 10pm-2am Fri & Sat; 🚌 13, 26, 40M

This is a relaxed but very serious jazz venue with excellent music from 10.30pm to 12.30am. Talent is both foreign and home grown.

### ☆ BOHEMIAN LOUNGE
Live Music
☎ 2526 6099; 3-5 Old Bailey St, Soho; ☉ 4pm-12.30am Mon-Wed, 4pm-2 or 3am Thu-Sat, happy hour 5-9pm; 🚌 13, 26, 40M

With suitably bohemian décor and regular tarot readings this is a great place for a libation any time

### ⓨ STAUNTON'S WINE BAR & CAFE Wine Bar & Café
☎ 2973 6611; 10-12 Staunton St, Soho; ☉ 8.30am-2am midnight, happy hour 5-9pm; 🚌 13, 12, 26

Staunton's is swish, cool and on the ball with decent wine and a lovely terrace. For eats, there's light fare downstairs and a modern international restaurant called Scirocco above.

but try to make it on Thursday after 9pm or Friday or Saturday after 10pm when live jazz kicks in.

### ☆ C CLUB *Club*
☎ 2526 1139; basement, California Tower, 30-32 D'Aguilar St, Lan Kwai Fong; ⏱ 6pm-3am Mon-Fri, 9pm-late Sat, happy hour 6-9pm Mon-Fri; Ⓜ Central

This tiny club below Lan Kwai Fong reeks of loucheness and is very popular for its quality cocktails, sexy house music and hip-hop, velvet cushions and the cheeky double bed in the alcove in the corner

### ☆ CALIFORNIA FITNESS
*Heath & Fitness*
☎ 2522 5229; www.californiafitness .com; ground fl, 1 Wellington St, Central; ⏱ 6am-midnight Mon-Sat, 8am-10pm Sun; Ⓜ Central

Asia's largest health club and fitness chain has seven outlets, including this one in Central.

### ☆ CAVERN *Live Music*
☎ 2121 8969; Shop 1, lower ground fl, Lan Kwai Fong Tower, 33 Wyndham St, Lan Kwai Fong (enter from D'Aguilar St); ⏱ 5pm-2am, happy hour 5-9pm; Ⓜ Central

Hong Kong's first (and still only) supper club, the Cavern is effectively a showcase for tribute bands, usually vintage 1960s.

Music from 8pm (7.30pm Sunday) is unplugged at 11pm (10.30pm Sunday).

### ☆ CLUB 97 *Club*
☎ 2186 1897; ground fl, Cosmos Bldg, 9-11 Lan Kwai Fong, Lan Kwai Fong ⏱ 6pm-2am Mon-Thu, 6pm-4am Fri, 8pm-4am Sat & Sun, happy hour 6-9pm Mon-Thu & Sat, 6-10pm Fri, 8-10pm Sun; Ⓜ Central

This schmoozy lounge bar has a popular happy hour (it's a gay event on Friday night) and there's salsa on Wednesday. Club 97 has a 'members only' policy to turn away the under-dressed, so make an effort.

### ☆ DK AROMATHERAPY
*Heath & Fitness*
☎ 2771 2847; www.aroma.com.hk; ground fl, 16A Staunton St, Soho; ⏱ 11am-10pm; 🚌 12, 13, 26

This is the place to come to, if you're looking for value for scents. Full-body aromatherapy treatments cost from $500 to $550.

### ☆ DROP *Club*
☎ 2543 8856, 2543 9230; basement, On Lok Mansion, 39-43 Hollywood Rd, Central (enter from Cochrane St); ⏱ 7pm-2am Tue, to 3am Wed, to 4am Thu, to 5am Fri, 10pm-5am Sat, 9pm-2am Sun, happy hour 7-10pm Tue-Fri; 🚌 13, 26, 40M

Pedestrians at Hong Kong's Zoological and Botanical Gardens (p45)

Deluxe lounge action, excellent tunes and potent cocktails keep Drop strong – though perhaps not quite as strong as it was – on the scene. The members-only policy after 11pm Thursday to Saturday is enforced to keep the dance-floor capacity at a manageable 'in like sardines' level.

### ⭐ FRINGE CLUB, THEATRE & STUDIO
藝穗會 *Live Music & Theatre*
☎ 2521 7251, theatre bookings 2521 9126; www.hkfringeclub.com; ground fl & 1st fl, Fringe Club, Dairy Farm Bldg, 2 Lower Albert Rd, Central; theatre tickets $100-

300; ⏲ noon-midnight Mon-Thu, noon-3am Fri & Sat, happy hour 3-9pm Mon-Thu, 3-8pm Fri & Sat; Ⓜ Central (exit G)
The Fringe, a friendly and eclectic venue on the border of the Lan Kwai Fong quadrant, has original music in its gallery-bar from 10.30pm on Friday and Saturday, with jazz, rock and world music getting the most airplay. There's a pleasant rooftop bar open in the warmer months. The intimate theatres, each seating up to a hundred, host eclectic local and international performances in English and Cantonese. There's also a pottery gallery.

NEIGHBOURHOODS

LAN KWAI FONG & SOHO

## ⭐ HAPPY FOOT REFLEXOLOGY CENTRE
知足樂 *Health & Fitness*

☎ 2544 1010; 11th & 13th fl, Jade Centre, 98-102 Wellington St, Central; ⊙ 10am-midnight; Ⓜ Central

Give your walk-weary tootsies (or other bits and pieces) a pampering at the aptly named Happy Foot. Foot/body massages start at $198/250 for 50 minutes. A pedicure costs $160.

## ⭐ HOME *Club*

☎ 2545 0023; 2nd fl, 23 Hollywood Rd, Central; ⊙ 10pm-3am Mon-Fri, 10pm-9am Sat, happy hour midnight-3am Wed & Thu; 🚌 13, 26, 40M

A meet 'n' greet and more for the styled and/or beautiful early on, this place turns into a bump 'n' grind later. With chill beds and a bouncy castle floor – well, anything goes. It's still partying well after dawn.

## ⭐ JOYCE IS NOT HERE
*Live Music*

☎ 2851 2999; 38-44 Peel St, Soho; ⊙ 11am-late Tue-Fri, 10am-late Sat & Sun, happy hour 4-8pm; 🚌 13, 26, 40M

'James or Ma?' we asked, trying to be clever. Alas, neither but this superchilled café-bar in reds, whites and blacks has something for everyone – from poetry readings and live music on Thursday to

Double-decker tramcar, Western Market tram terminus (p194)

booze and Sunday brunch. Love the place.

## ⭐ PROPAGANDA *Club*

☎ 2868 1316; lower ground fl, 1 Hollywood Rd, Central; admission $20-200 Fri & Sat; ⊙ 9pm-4am Tue-Thu, 9pm-6am Fri & Sat; 🚌 13, 26, 40M

This is Hong Kong's premier gay dance club (and meat market). Cover charges apply on Friday and Saturday. Enter from Ezra's Lane, which runs between Pottinger and Cochrane Sts.

### ⭐ PURE FITNESS
*Heath & Fitness*

☎ 2970 3366; www.pure-fit.com; 1st, 2nd & 3rd fl, Kinwick Centre, 32 Hollywood Rd, Soho; ⏱ 6am-midnight Mon-Sat, 8am-10pm Sun; Ⓜ Central
Enter this favourite of the Soho set from Shelley St. There is also a branch at Two IFC (p49).

### ⭐ SENSE OF TOUCH
*Health & Fitness*

☎ 2869 0939; lower ground floor, The Ovolo, 2 Arbuthnot Rd, Soho; ⏱ 10.30am-8.30pm Mon-Fri, 10.30am-7pm Sat, 10.30am-6pm Sun; 🚌 13, 26, 40M
This award-winning spa offers every conceivable form of treatment (cappuccino wrap, anyone?) but most are Asian in origin, including ayurvedic massage ($580 per hour) and Thai hot-poultice therapy.

### ⭐ WORKS *Club*

☎ 2868 6102; 1st fl, 30-32 Wyndham St, Soho; tickets $60-100 Fri & Sat; ⏱ 7pm-2am, happy hour 7-10.30pm Mon-Sat; Ⓜ Central
Sister club to Propaganda (opposite), Works is where most people – on the prowl or otherwise – start an evening on the town. Pay the weekend cover here and you'll get into Propaganda.

### ⭐ YOGA FITNESS
*Health & Fitness*

☎ 2851 8353; www.yoga-fitness.com; 5th fl, Sea Bird House, 22-28 Wyndham St, Central; Ⓜ Central
If you just can't get away from bending and stretching, Yoga Fitness place offers hatha instruction for $140 per class or $499 for five classes. See the website for information on opening hours and classes. There's also the excellent Yoga Kitchen with all sorts of healthy goodies.

### ⭐ YUMLA *Club*

☎ 2147 2383; lower basement, 79 Wyndham St, Central (enter from Pottinger St); ⏱ 5pm-2am Mon-Thu, 5pm-4am Fri & Sat, 7pm-2am Sun, happy hour 5-9pm Mon-Sat, 7-9pm Sun; 🚌 13, 26, 40M
This place below chilled Soda (p68) is arguably the hippest and least pretentious club in Hong Kong, with a cool crowd and excellent tunes. Watch out for the murals.

# SEE

## HONG KONG MUSEUM OF MEDICAL SCIENCES
### 香港醫學博物館

☎ 2549 5123; www.hkmms.org.hk; 2 Caine Lane, the Mid-Levels; adult/child $10/5; ⏱ 10am-5pm Tue-Sat, 1-5pm Sun; 🚌 3B, 23, 23B, 40, 40M, 103, green minibus 8 (from GPO)

This small museum of medical implements and accoutrements is less interesting for its exhibits than for its architecture and attached herbal garden. It is housed in what was once the Old Pathological Institute, an Edwardian-style brick-and-tile structure built in 1905. The exhibits comparing Chinese and Western approaches to medicine are unusual and instructive.

## MADAME TUSSAUD'S
### 香港杜沙夫人蠟像館

☎ 2849 6966; www.madame-tussauds.com.hk; Shop P101, Level P1, Peak Tower, 128 Peak Rd, the Peak; adult/child Mon-Fri $115/65, Sat & Sun $120/70; ⏱ 10am-10pm; 🚋 Peak Tram 🚌 15

Most people go to the Peak for the views (p74) or the thrill of ascending Hong Kong's highest point at a preposterous incline on the Peak Tram (p195). But there are some other lures, including this attraction in the Peak Tower, with eerie (and scary) wax likenesses of

---

### HONG KONG MUSEUMS PASS

The **Hong Kong Museums Pass** (admission 7 days $30, adult/senior & student 6 months $50/25, 1 year $100/50) allows multiple entries to six of Hong Kong's museums: Hong Kong Museum of Coastal Defence, Hong Kong Science Museum, Hong Kong Museum of History, Hong Kong Museum of Art, Hong Kong Space Museum (excluding the Space Theatre) and the Hong Kong Heritage Museum. They are available from any Hong Kong Tourism Board (HKTB) outlet (p200) and the participating museums.

---

international stars as well as local celebrities such as Jackie Chan, Andy Lau, Michelle Yeoh, Aaron Kwok and Cecilia Cheung. There are also packages available.

## OHEL LEAH SYNAGOGUE

☎ 2589 2621; www.ohelleah.org; 70 Robinson Rd, the Mid-Levels; admission free; ⏱ 10.30am-7pm Mon-Thu; 🚌 3B, 13, 23, 23B, 40

This 'Moorish Romantic' temple, completed in 1902, is named after Leah Gubbay Sassoon, matriarch of a wealthy (and philanthropic) Sephardic Jewish family that can trace its roots back to the beginning of the colony. Bring your passport and expect a thorough security check if you plan to visit the sumptuous interior.

**Poon Ka-Kui,**
*Photographer & owner of Photo Scientific (p61)*

**New or old technology:** A digital camera is easy to operate and replaces the brain. **Who's buying what:** 70% of sales are digital and 30% film, though among those who want to be true to the art of photography, it's almost an even split. **What's in the future:** The principles remain the same – box, aperture, speed, distance. Taking a good photograph will still require both commonsense and creativity. **What's to miss about Hong Kong:** The noise – it's way too quiet outside! **Chopsticks or knife and fork:** Chopsticks, especially old-fashioned Cantonese. **Perfect day out:** I'd go up to the Peak and then down to the Western District. I'd take the tram to Shau Kei Wan, slowly viewing the city as it goes past. I'd spend a romantic evening in the streets of Stanley.

# 🍴 EAT

The Peak Tower has undergone extensive renovations recently and now has a dozen eateries, including one of Hong Kong's finest new restaurants with the best view in town.

### 🍴 CAFE DECO *International* $$$
☎ 2849 5111; levels 1 & 2, Peak Galleria, 118 Peak Rd, the Peak; 🕙 11.30am-midnight Mon-Thu, 11.30am-1am Fri & Sat, 9.30am-midnight Sun; 🚋 Peak Tram 🚌 15

Most punters would be content with the views, live jazz (7pm to 11pm Thursday to Saturday) and stylish Art Deco furnishings. But the eclectic menu – offering everything from the simple but fresh (oysters, sushi) to more complex bistro and Indian dishes – is way above average. Don't miss the extraordinary weekend brunch (11.30am to 2.30pm).

### 🍴 EATING PLUS
*International, Asian* $
☎ 2849 7855; Shop P101, level P1, Peak Tower, 128 Peak Rd, the Peak; 🕙 11.30am-10pm; 🚋 Peak Tram 🚌 15

Style comes cheap at this very vogue eatery in the Peak Tower.

On the Peak Tram

Omelettes are fluffy, juices freshly squeezed and lunch and dinner extend to soups, noodles (a successful mix of East and West) and rice dishes, including risotto.

### 🍴 PEAK LOOKOUT
*International, Asian* $$$

☎ 2849 1000; 121 Peak Rd, the Peak; 🕑 10.30am-midnight Mon-Fri, 8.30am-1am Sat, 8.30am-midnight Sun; 🚋 Peak Tram 🚌 15

East meets West at this colonial-style restaurant, with everything from Indian and French to Thai and Italian on offer. Stick to the oysters (a dozen varieties), the barbecue and the views, which are to the south of the island, not over the harbour.

### 🍴 PEARL ON THE PEAK
*International, Fusion* $$$$

☎ 2849 5123, 2101 1268; level P1, Peak Tower, 128 Peak Rd, the Peak; 🕑 11.30am-midnight Mon-Fri, 9am-midnight Sat & Sun; 🚋 Peak Tram 🚌 15

This welcome addition to the revamped Peak Tower has award winning Australian chef Geoff Lindsay at the helm, which

suggests Asian hints and Middle Eastern whispers. The stunning views come though loud and clear.

### 🍴 PHOENIX
*International, Modern British* $$$

☎ 2546 2110; 29 Shelley St, the Mid-Levels; 🕑 4-11pm Mon-Thu, 11am-11pm Fri, 9am-11pm Sat & Sun; 🚌 12, 13, 23A

This little gastropub, alongside the Central Escalator, serves mostly modern British comfort food with vague flavours of the Mediterranean (is it global warming?) thrown in for good measure. It's a great place for weekend brunch (9am to 4pm).

### 🍴 TAI WOO
太湖海鮮城 *Cantonese* $$

☎ 2548 4289; 92 Caine Rd, the Mid-Levels; 🕑 10am-11pm; 🚌 3B, 23

If you're anxious to try old-style Cantonese cooking at its finest, look no further than the 'Great Lake'. The large crab dumplings are out of this world and you might also try the stewed grouper fin and roast pigeon. There's also a branch in Causeway Bay.

# >HONG KONG ISLAND: ADMIRALTY & WAN CHAI

You might not even have noticed Admiralty as a district were it not for the dominating Pacific Place shopping centre and several modern buildings of note, including the blindingly gold Far East Finance Centre, which is at 16 Harcourt Rd, and known locally as 'Amah's Tooth', a reference to the traditional Chinese maids' preference for gold fillings and caps. Think of it as the gateway to Hong Kong Island's most famous district, Wan Chai (Little Bay). Although Wan Chai had a reputation during the Vietnam War as an anything-goes red-light district, today it is mainly a centre for shopping, business and more upmarket entertainment. If you want to see how far Wan Chai has come, check out the fortresslike Hong Kong Convention & Exhibition Centre. The southeastern part of Wan Chai retains some of its old character, with all sorts of traditional shops, markets and workshops.

## ADMIRALTY & WAN CHAI

### ◎ SEE
Flagstaff House Museum
of Tea Ware...................... 1 B5
Happy Valley
Racecourse....................... 2 D1
Hong Kong Convention &
Exhibition Centre .......... 3 B3
Hong Kong Park ............. 4 C6
Hong Kong Racing
Museum ........................... 5 D1
KS Lo Gallery ................. 6 B5
Lovers' Rock .................... 7 D2
Pao Galleries .................. 8 B3

### ⬚ SHOP
Cosmos Books.................. 9 C3
Design Gallery .............. 10 B3
Hong Kong Records .... (see 11)
Kelly & Walsh .............. (see 11)
Kent & Curwen........... (see 11)
King & Country .......... (see 11)
Pacific Custom Tailors .. (see 11)

Pacific Place.................. 11 C4
Vivienne Tam............. (see 11)
Watson's Wine
Cellar .......................... (see 11)
Wise Kids .................... (see 11)

### 🍴 EAT
369 Shanghai
Restaurant ..................... 12 B3
American Restaurant .... 13 B3
Beijing Shui Jiao
Wong .............................. 14 B3
Café Too ........................ 15 C5
Carrianna Chiu Chow
Restaurant ..................... 16 B2
Che's Cantonese
Restaurant ..................... 17 B3
One Harbour Road.......... 18 B3
Petrus ............................. 19 C5
R66 .................................. 20 C3
Steak Expert ................. 21 C3
Thai Basil .................... (see 11)
Yé Shanghai ............... (see 11)

### 🍷 DRINK
Bar 109.......................... 22 B3
Champagne Bar ............ 23 B3
Delaney's ...................... 24 B3
Devil's Advocate........... 25 B3
Maya .............................. 26 B3
Mes Amis ....................... 27 B3

### ★ PLAY
1/5 .................................. 28 C4
Agnès B Cinema............. 29 B3
Cine-Art House.............. 30 B2
Dusk till Dawn .............. 31 B3
Hong Kong Academy for
Performing Arts........... 32 B3
Hong Kong Arts Centre.... 33 B3
Joe Banana's................. 34 B3
Neptune Disco II........... 35 B3
Tribeca .......................... 36 B3
Wanch ............................ 37 B3

NEIGHBOURHOODS

TSIM SHA TSUI & TSIM SHA TSUI EAST

Lobby of Peninsula Hotel Hong Kong (p115)

## 🍴 SABATINI *Italian* $$$$

☎ 2721 5215; 3rd fl, Royal Garden Hotel, 69 Mody Rd, Tsim Sha Tsui East; ⏱ noon-2.30pm & 6-11pm; Ⓜ Tsim Sha Tsui 🚢 Tsim Sha Tsui East Ferry Pier 🚌 5, 8
One of the finest Italian eateries in Hong Kong, classy Sabatini has murals on the walls and ceilings and polished terracotta tiles on the floor. Even classic Italian dishes, such as fettuccine carbonara, come across as light in the best sense, leaving room to sample the exquisite desserts.

## 🍴 SPRING DEER
鹿鳴春飯店
*Northern Chinese* $$

☎ 2366 4012; 1st fl, Lyton Bldg, 42 Mody Rd, Tsim Sha Tsui; ⏱ 11.30am-3pm & 6-11pm; Ⓜ Tsim Sha Tsui
Probably Hong Kong's most famous (if not most salubrious) Northern Chinese restaurant, the Spring Deer serves some of the crispiest Peking duck in town for the cost of $280 per bird. The restaurant is extremely popular, so be sure to book in advance.

NEIGHBOURHOODS

ADMIRALTY & WAN CHAI

# ⊙ SEE

## ⊙ HONG KONG CONVENTION & EXHIBITION CENTRE
香港會議展覽中心

☎ 2582 8888; www.hkcec.com; 1 Expo Dr, Wan Chai; admission free; 🚌 18 Ⓜ Wan Chai

This enormous complex, built in 1988 and extended onto reclaimed land for the handover ceremony in 1997, boasts an enormous 'glass curtain' – a window seven storeys high – facing the harbour. On the waterfront promenade to the northeast is the **Golden Bauhinia**, a 6m-tall statue of Hong Kong's symbol marking the establishment of the Hong Kong SAR.

## ⊙ HONG KONG PARK
香港公園

☎ 2521 5041; www.lcsd.gov.hk/parks /hkp/en/index.php; 19 Cotton Tree Dr, Admiralty; admission free; 🕑 park 6am-11pm, conservatory & aviary 9am-5pm, tours 8-10am Wed; 🚌 12A Ⓜ Admiralty (exit C1) 👤

We like to visit the park primarily to walk among our fine feathered friends at their level (left), but there are a couple of other draw-cards here, including the **Flagstaff House Museum of Tea Ware** (☎ 2869 0690; www.lcsd.gov.hk/CE/Museum /Arts/english/tea/intro/eintro.html; 10 Cotton Tree Dr, Admiralty; admission free; 🕑 10am-5pm Wed-Mon) housed in the oldest colonial building (1846) extant in Hong Kong. It contains a collection of antique Chinese tea ware. Next door the **KS Lo Gallery** (same hours as the museum) contains rare Chinese ceramics and stone seals collected by the gallery's eponymous benefactor. There is also a squash and sports centre for those inclined.

---

### WORTH THE TRIP

Just south of Wan Chai and accessible by tram from Hennessy Rd is the famous **Happy Valley Racecourse** (☎ 2895 1523, 2966 8111; www.happyvalleyracecourse.com; 2 Sports Rd, Happy Valley; tickets $10, short-stay adult tourist tickets $100-150; from 7pm Wed Sep-early Jul; 🚌 75, 90, 97), where you might spend an exciting evening watching the gee-gees go through their paces or, by day, have a look at the esoteric but complete **Hong Kong Racing Museum** (☎ 2966 8065; www.hkjc.com/english /museum/mu02_index.htm; 2nd fl, Happy Valley Stand, Wong Nai Chung Rd; admission free; 🕑 meeting days 10am-5pm, Tue-Sun 10am-12.30pm). A kilometre or so west of the racecourse is **Lovers' Rock** (off Bowen Rd, Wan Chai Gap; admission free; 🕑 24hr; 🚌 15, 15B), a phallus-shaped boulder on a bluff above Bowen Rd that is a favourite pilgrimage site for childless women.

**John Batten,**
*Gallery owner & organiser of Hong Kong Art Walk (p29)*

**Hong Kong in the art world:** There's no passion for art, no patrons who will support a noncommercial enterprise – it's a city with no memory. **That bad?** At any one time there are one or two really good shows on but you have to sift through a lot. **Place to go for serious local art:** Talk to artists and visit their studios – most galleries just show decorative art. **Worth a second look:** The Art Museum at the Chinese University of Hong Kong. **Day out:** A walk through the back streets of old Mong Kok with a stop at Mido (p134). **Chopsticks or knife and fork:** Chopsticks, especially Chiu Chow food. **Hong Kong in a word:** Vibrant – it's always happening if you can cut through the hype.

## WHEN THE CHIPS WERE DOWN

The most important event in the history of the Happy Valley Racecourse – individual winnings notwithstanding – was the huge fire in 1918 that killed hundreds of people. Many of the victims were buried in the cemeteries that surround the track. The disaster is evocatively described in Robert Elegant's *Dynasty*, a doorstop epic novel about Hong Kong.

### ◉ PAO GALLERIES
包氏畫廊
☎ 2824 5330; www.hkac.org.hk; 2 Harbour Rd, Wan Chai; admission free; 🕐 during exhibitions 10am-6pm; 🚌 12 Ⓜ Wan Chai (exit A1)

This major contemporary art gallery in the Hong Kong Arts Centre (p93) hosts retrospectives and group shows in all visual media spread out over two levels. The curatorial vision is lively without being too provocative. After all, this is Hong Kong.

# 🛍 SHOP

### ◻ COSMOS BOOKS
天地圖書 *Books*
☎ 2866 1677; basement & 1st fl, 30 Johnston Rd, Wan Chai; 🕐 10am-8pm; Ⓜ Wan Chai (exit A3) 🈂

This outlet has a good selection of China-related books in the basement. Upstairs there are English-language books (a large selection of nonfiction) plus one of the city's best stationery departments.

### ◻ DESIGN GALLERY
*Gifts & Souvenirs*
☎ 2584 4146; www.hkdesigngallery .com; Hong Kong Convention & Exhibition Centre, 1 Harbour Rd, Wan Chai; 🕐 10am-7.30pm Mon-Fri, 10am-7pm Sat, noon-7.30pm Sun; 🚌 18 Ⓜ Wan Chai

Supported by the Hong Kong Trade Development Council, this shop showcases Hong Kong design in the form of jewellery, toys, ornaments and gadgets. It's a somewhat chaotic – but often rewarding – gaggle of goodies.

### ◻ HONG KONG RECORDS
香港唱片 *Music*
☎ 2845 7088, 2530 9696; Shop 253, 2nd fl, Pacific Place, 88 Queensway, Admiralty; 🕐 10am-8.30pm Mon-Thu, 10am-9pm Fri-Sun; Ⓜ Admiralty 🈂

If you're looking for something different, this local outfit has a good selection of local and international sounds, including traditional Chinese, jazz, classical and contemporary music. It also offers a good range of DVDs of both Chinese films and Western movies with Chinese subtitles. Make sure they work for your DVD region.

### 🏠 KELLY & WALSH *Books*
☎ 2522 5743; www.kellyandwalsh
.com; Shop 236, 2nd fl, Pacific Place, 88
Queensway, Admiralty; 🕙 10.30am-8pm
Sun-Thu, 10.30am-8.30pm Fri & Sat;
Ⓜ Admiralty 🚻

This smart shop has a great choice
of art, design and culinary books
and the staff know the stock well.
The children's books are shelved in
a handy kids' reading lounge.

### 🏠 KENT & CURWEN
*Clothing & Accessories*
☎ 2840 0023; Shop 224, 2nd fl,
Pacific Place, 88 Queensway, Admiralty;
🕙 10am-8pm Sun-Thu, 10am-9pm Fri &
Sat; Ⓜ Admiralty 🚻

Distinguished suits, dress shirts,
ties, cufflinks and casual tops for
the gentleman who'd rather look
to the manor born than arriviste
broke.

---

**SALE ON**

Winter sales are held during the first
three weeks of January and summer
sales in late June and early July. Hong
Kong pretties itself up for Fashion
Week, the industry's most important
annual event, in mid-January (fall
and winter) and mid-July (spring and
summer). The main parades and events
take place at the Hong Kong Convention and Exhibition Centre (p82) in Wan
Chai, but keep an eye out for shows and
shindigs in shopping malls around the
territory.

---

### 🏠 KING & COUNTRY
*Gifts & Souvenirs*
☎ 2525 8603; www.kingandcountry.com;
Shop 362, 3rd fl, Pacific Place, 88 Queens-
way, Admiralty; 🕙 10.30am-8.30pm Mon-
Sat, 11am-7pm Sun; Ⓜ Admiralty 🚻

This has models and miniatures
(mostly military, the American War
of Independence, Napoleonic Wars
etc), but also street models of old
Hong Kong: building frontages, a
Chinese wedding procession, even
an '*amah* (maid) with baby and
chicken'. They're fast becoming
coveted collectors' items.

### 🏠 PACIFIC CUSTOM TAILORS
*Clothing & Accessories*
☎ 2845 5377; Shop 113, 1st fl, Pacific Place,
88 Queensway, Admiralty; 🕙 9.30am-
7.30pm Mon-Sat; Ⓜ Admiralty 🚻

This is our favourite bespoke tailor
in Hong Kong, wrapping us in new
duds many times. They'll make
or copy anything; turnaround on
most items is two or three days,
including two fittings. Excellent,
personable service.

### 🏠 VIVIENNE TAM
*Clothing & Accessories*
☎ 2918 0238; www.viviennetam
.com; Shop 209, 2nd fl, Pacific Place,
88 Queensway, Admiralty; 🕙 11am-
8.30pm Sun-Thu, 11am-9pm Fri & Sat;
Ⓜ Admiralty 🚻

Sophisticated yet adventurous
women's wear from New York ▶

NEIGHBOURHOODS

ADMIRALTY & WAN CHAI

Store in Pacific Place shopping centre

based designer Vivienne Tam, who
was trained in Hong Kong.

### WATSON'S WINE CELLAR
**WATSON'S** 酒窖 *Food & Drink*
☎ 2526 2832; www.watsonswine
.com; Great Food Hall, lower ground fl,
Pacific Place, 88 Queensway, Admiralty;
🕑 10.30am-10pm; Ⓜ Admiralty 🚇
The choice at this wine emporium
in the basement of Pacific Place is
enormous and the knowledgeable
staff are always willing to assist
and advise.

### WISE KIDS *Toys*
☎ 2868 0133; www.wisekidstoys.com;
Shop 134, 1st fl, Pacific Place, 88 Queensway, Admiralty; 🕑 10am-8pm Sun-Wed,
10am-9pm Thu-Sat; Ⓜ Admiralty 🚇
Nothing to plug in and nothing with batteries: Wise Kids
concentrates on kids generating
energy with what's upstairs. Along
with stuffed toys, card games and
things to build, there are practical
items for parents such as toilet-lid
locks and carry-alls.

# 🍴 EAT

## 🍴 369 SHANGHAI RESTAURANT

上海三六九飯店

*Shanghainese* $$

☎ 2527 2343; 30-32 O'Brien Rd, Wan Chai; 🕐 11am-4am; Ⓜ Wan Chai
Low-key Shanghainese eatery that's nothing like five-star but does the dumpling job well. It's family-run with good comfy booths in the front window and open late, for stumbling in after a night out on the Wanch. Try their signature hot and sour soup ($40).

## 🍴 AMERICAN RESTAURANT

美利堅京菜

*Northern Chinese* $$

☎ 2527 7277; ground fl, Golden Star Bldg, 20 Lockhart Rd, Wan Chai; 🕐 11am-11.30pm; Ⓜ Wan Chai
This place, which chose its name to lure American sailors on R&R through its doors during the Vietnam War, has been serving earthy Northern Chinese cuisine for over half a century. As you'd expect, the Peking duck ($275) and the beggar's chicken ($385) are tops.

## 🍴 BEIJING SHUI JIAO WONG

北京水餃皇

*Northern Chinese* $

☎ 2527 0289; 118 Jaffe Rd, Wan Chai; 🕐 7.30am-11pm Mon-Sat, 11am-11pm Sun; Ⓜ Wan Chai

The 'Dumpling King' serves the best (and cheapest) Northern-style dumplings, *guo tie* (pot stickers) and soup noodles in Hong Kong.

## 🍴 CAFÉ TOO *International* $$

☎ 2820 8571; 7th fl, Island Shangri-La Hong Kong, Pacific Place, Supreme Court Rd, Admiralty; 🕐 6.30am-1am; Ⓜ Admiralty
This immensely popular, beautifully designed food hall has a half-dozen kitchens preparing dishes from around the world and one of the best buffets in town. There are à la carte options and lighter fare such as sandwiches.

## 🍴 CARRIANNA CHIU CHOW RESTAURANT

佳寧娜潮州菜 *Chiu Chow* $$$

☎ 2511 1282; 1st fl, AXA Centre, 151 Gloucester Rd, Wan Chai (enter from Tonnochy Rd); 🕐 11am-11.30pm; Ⓜ Wan Chai
For Chiu Chow food, the Carrianna still rates very high after all these years. Try the cold dishes (sliced goose with vinegar, crab claws), pork with tofu or Chiu Chow-style chicken.

## 🍴 CHE'S CANTONESE RESTAURANT

車氏粵菜軒 *Cantonese* $$$

☎ 2528 1123; 4th fl, Broadway, 54-62 Lockhart Rd, Wan Chai; 🕐 11am-3pm & 6-11.30pm; Ⓜ Wan Chai

This excellent Cantonese restaurant serves many home-style delicacies and offers a special seasonal menu with a dozen additional dishes.

### 🍴 ONE HARBOUR ROAD
*Cantonese* $$$$

☎ 2588 1234; 8th fl, Grand Hyatt Hong Kong, 1 Harbour Rd, Wan Chai; ⏱ noon-2.30pm & 6.30-10.30pm; 🚌 18 Ⓜ Wan Chai

This is just about the classiest Chinese restaurant in Hong Kong. In addition to the beautiful design and fabulous harbour view, six pages of gourmet dishes await your perusal. Set lunches and dinners are good value.

### 🍴 PETRUS *French* $$$$

☎ 2820 8590; 56th fl, Island Shangri-La Hong Kong, Pacific Place, Supreme Court Rd, Admiralty; ⏱ noon-3pm & 6.30-11pm Mon-Sat; Ⓜ Admiralty

With its head (and prices, it must be said) in the clouds, Petrus is one of the finest restaurants in Hong Kong. Expect traditional (not nouvelle) French cuisine and stunning harbour views. Coat and tie required for guys.

### 🍴 R66
旋轉餐廳 *International* $$

☎ 2862 6166; 62nd fl, Hopewell Centre, 183 Queen's Rd E, Wan Chai; ⏱ noon-2.30pm, 3-5pm (tea) & 6.30-10pm; 🚌 6, 6X Ⓜ Wan Chai

---

**ON THE GO & TO GO**

You'll see signs for Cafe de Coral, Maxim's, Fairwood and Saint's Alp just about everywhere. These are local fast-food joints where you can get decent Chinese and Western meals on the hoof for very little. Among the best places for sandwiches, soups, salads, baked goods and fresh juices are branches of the Délifrance, Oliver's Super Sandwiches and Mix chains. 7-Eleven outlets, on virtually every corner of the territory and usually open 24 hours, are good places for drinks and snacks to take away.

---

R66 – it's on the 62nd, not the 66th floor – obeys the unwritten code of revolving restaurants by playing cheesy music and serving average buffets at reasonable prices, but you can't beat the view. To access the lipstick tube-like Hopewell Centre's out facing bubble lifts, change at the 17th floor (lifts are in the alcove opposite lift 6) and again on the 56th floor.

### 🍴 STEAK EXPERT
扒王之王 *Steakhouse* $

☎ 2528 0100; www.steakexpert.com .hk; 1st fl, Empire Hotel Hong Kong, 33 Hennessy Rd, Wan Chai (enter from Fenwick St); ⏱ 7am-midnight Mon-Sat, 10am-midnight Sun; Ⓜ Wan Chai

OK, so it's part of a chain. But the steaks are excellent value for what they serve, and this branch is in the heart of Wan Chai and keeps very long (and relatively late) hours. Just watch out for the pepper sauce.

### 🍴 THAI BASIL *Thai* $$

☎ 2537 4682; Shop 005, lower ground fl, Pacific Place, 88 Queensway, Admiralty; 🕒 11.30am-10.45pm; Ⓜ Admiralty 🏮

This restaurant in a mall basement (did he say mall basement?) turns out some surprisingly authentic (and quite lovely) Thai dishes. This may not be a destination but it's not a bad pit stop while shopping.

### 🍴 YÈ SHANGHAI

夜上海 *Shanghainese* $$

☎ 2918 9833; Shop 332, Level 3, Pacific Place, 88 Queensway, Admiralty; 🕒 11.30am-3pm & 6-11.30pm; Ⓜ Admiralty 🏮

With a sister restaurant in Shanghai, this is almost street-level Shanghainese cuisine but with a few tweaks. The cold drunken pigeon is a Shao Xing wine-soaked winner and the steamed dumplings are perfectly plump, but sometimes this restaurant goes for clatter over substance. There's live music from 9pm to 11pm Thursday to Saturday.

Restaurant diners

# ⧖ DRINK

*Nov 7/08. Wow, unending stripper bars*

Wan Chai is part sleaze territory, with awful hostess bars along Lockhart Rd, and part upbeat fun, with lots of zippy club action and late-night cover-band venues at the western ends of Jaffe and Lockhart Rds. It's the part of town that kicks on latest – handy if dawn is approaching and you still want more.

## ⧖ BAR 109 *Bar*

☎ 2861 3336; 109 Lockhart Rd;
🕑 noon-3am, happy hour 3-9pm;
Ⓜ Wan Chai

Tired of rubbing, er, shoulders with working girls in the Wanch? Well, even if not, the 109 will give you 110 reasons to flock here. It's a serious chill-out zone cobbled from a 1920s-vintage bakery and divided into three sections, including a bar, a covered 'outside' area and a 1st-floor balcony.

## ⧖ CHAMPAGNE BAR
*Live Music Bar*

☎ 2588 1234 ext 7321; ground fl, Grand Hyatt Hong Kong, 1 Harbour Rd, Wan Chai; 🕑 5pm-1am; Ⓜ Wan Chai

Take your fizz in the sumptuous surrounds of the Grand Hyatt's Champagne Bar, kitted out in Art Deco furnishings realistic enough to evoke the Paris of the 1920s. Live blues or jazz rings through the bar most evenings, and the circular main bar is always busy.

Bar at Grand Hyatt Hong Kong, Wan Chai

### ▼ DELANEY'S *Bar*
☎ 2804 2880; ground & 1st fl, One Capital Place, 18 Luard Rd, Wan Chai; ⏰ noon-3am, happy hour noon-9pm; Ⓜ Wan Chai

At this immensely popular Irish watering hole you can choose between the ground floor pub tiled in black and white, or the sports bar and restaurant on the 1st floor. There's also a branch in Tsim Sha Tsui.

### ▼ DEVIL'S ADVOCATE *Bar*
☎ 2865 7271; 48-50 Lockhart Rd, Wan Chai; ⏰ noon-late Mon-Sat, 1pm-late Sun, happy hour noon-9pm daily & midnight-1am Fri & Sat; Ⓜ Wan Chai

This pleasant pub in the thick of things in Wan Chai is as relaxed as they come. The bar spills on to the pavement and the staff are charming.

### ▼ MAYA *Bar*
☎ 2866 6200; 68-70 Lockhart Rd, Wan Chai; ⏰ 11am-2am Sun-Thu, 11am-3am Fri & Sat, happy hour noon-9pm; Ⓜ Wan Chai

This lovely new bar has a name that apparently means 'illusion' in Sanskrit. It's a design-minded oasis in Wan Chai. We love the bold black-and-white patterns on the wall, the bright red bar and of course the (almost) never-ending happy/relaxing/two-for-one hour(s).

### ▼ MES AMIS *Bar & Wine Bar*
☎ 2527 6680; 83 Lockhart Rd, Wan Chai; ⏰ noon-2.30am Sun-Tue & Thu, noon-5am Wed, noon-6am Fri & Sat, happy hour 4-9pm Mon-Thu, noon-9pm Sat & Sun; Ⓜ Wan Chai

This easygoing bar may be in the lap – so to speak – of girly club land but is poles (again, as it were) apart. It has a good range of wines and a Mediterranean-style snack list. There's a DJ from 11pm on Wednesday, Friday and Saturday night.

## ⭐ PLAY

### ⭐ 1/5 *Club*
☎ 2520 2515; 1st fl, Starcrest Bldg, 9 Star St, Wan Chai; ⏰ 6pm-3am Mon-Thu, 6pm-4am Fri, 9pm-5am Sat, happy hour 6-9pm Mon-Fri; Ⓜ Admiralty

Pronounced 'one-fifth', this lounge bar–club has a broad bar backed by a two-storey drinks selection from which bar staff concoct some of Hong Kong's best cocktails. Thursday is salsa night.

### ⭐ AGNÈS B CINEMA *Cinema*
☎ 2582 0200; www.hkac.org.hk; upper basement, Hong Kong Arts Centre, 2 Harbour Rd, Wan Chai; 🚌 18 Ⓜ Wan Chai

Despite its branded name, this very uncommercial cinema is *the* place for classics, revivals, alternative screenings and travelling film festivals.

Neon sign for Neptune Disco II

### ⭐ CINE-ART HOUSE
影藝 *Cinema*

☎ 2827 4820; www.cityline.com.hk /eng/venues/cine_art.jsp; ground fl, Sun Hung Kai Centre, 30 Harbour Rd, Wan Chai; tickets $55; 🚌 18 Ⓜ Wan Chai
This alternative cinema specialises in English-language films but it's become a real hit-or-miss affair these days.

### ⭐ DUSK TILL DAWN *Live Music*
☎ 2528 4689; 76-84 Jaffe Rd, Wan Chai; 🕐 noon-7am Mon-Fri, 3pm-7am Sat & Sun, happy hour 5-9pm; Ⓜ Wan Chai
Live music from 10.30pm, with an emphasis on beats and vibes that will get your booty shaking. The dance floor can be packed but the atmosphere is more friendly than sleazy. The food sticks to easy fillers such as meat pies and burgers.

### ⭐ HONG KONG ACADEMY FOR PERFORMING ARTS
香港演藝學院
*Theatre, Dance, Music*

☎ 2584 8500, bookings 3128 8288; www.hkapa.edu; 1 Gloucester Rd, Wan Chai; performances $80-750; Ⓜ Wan Chai 🚇
Stages local and overseas performances of dance, drama and music. The building (1985), with its striking triangular atrium and exterior Meccano-like frame, was designed by local architect Simon Kwan.

## ⭐ HONG KONG ARTS CENTRE
香港藝術中心 *Theatre*

☎ 2582 0200; www.hkac.org.hk; 2 Harbour Rd, Wan Chai; performances $80-400; 🚌 18 Ⓜ Wan Chai

This independent contemporary arts centre showcases home-grown talent and its Shouson Theatre hosts drama (often in English). The centre also publishes a monthly listings magazine called *Artslink*. See also Pao Galleries (p84) and Agnès B Cinema (p91).

## ⭐ JOE BANANA'S *Club*

☎ 2529 1811; ground fl, Shiu Lam Bldg, 23 Luard Rd, Wan Chai; 🕐 noon-5am Mon-Thu, noon-6am Fri, 4pm-6am Sat, 4pm-5am Sun, happy hour 6-10pm; Ⓜ Wan Chai

JB's, in Wan Chai forever (or at least since we were bopping and grooving), has dropped its long-standing wet T-shirt/boxers aesthetic and gone for more of a bamboo-bar feel. The dancing is good and it's always a fun night out.

## ⭐ NEPTUNE DISCO II *Club*

☎ 2865 2238; basement, 98 Jaffe Rd, Wan Chai; men/women Sun $100/70; 🕐 4pm-6am Mon-Fri, 2pm-6am Sat & Sun, happy hour 4-9pm Mon-Fri, 2-9pm Sat; Ⓜ Wan Chai

Neptune II is a fun club with a mostly Filipino crowd and a rockin' covers band. If everything's closing and you can't bear to stop bopping, this is the place to head for. It really rocks at the Sunday afternoon-tea dance starting at 2pm.

## ⭐ TRIBECA *Club*

☎ 2836 3690; 4th fl, Renaissance Harbour View Hotel, 1 Harbour Rd, Wan Chai; men $120; 🕐 6pm-4am Mon-Fri, 10pm-late Sat, happy hour 6pm-midnight Mon-Wed & Fri, 6-9pm Thu; 🚌 18 Ⓜ Wan Chai

No, not NYC but glitzy Hong Kong… It's an *über*-decked-out club with chatting lounges, a long bar and popular theme nights (eg salsa on Sunday). It's popular with a suave Cantonese crowd, so dress to impress. There's free entry and drinks for women on Thursday night.

## ⭐ WANCH *Live Music*

☎ 2861 1621; 54 Jaffe Rd, Wan Chai; 🕐 11am-3am Mon-Fri, 2pm-3am Sat & Sun, happy hour 11am-10pm Mon-Fri, 2-10pm Sat & Sun; Ⓜ Wan Chai

The Wanch has live music (mostly rock and folk) happening seven nights a week from 9pm or 10pm, with the occasional solo guitarist thrown in to the mix. Jam night is Wednesday at 9pm. If you're not here for the music, well, the Wanch is also a serious pulling place.

# >HONG KONG ISLAND: CAUSEWAY BAY

Causeway Bay, called Tung Lo Wan (Copper Gong Bay) in Cantonese, was the site of a British settlement in the 1840s. It was also once an area of *godowns* (a Hong Kong business or pidgin English word for warehouses), and a well-protected harbour for fisherfolk and boatpeople. The new Causeway Bay, one of Hong Kong's top shopping areas, was built up from swampland and sand from the bottom of the harbour. Jardine Matheson, one of Hong Kong's largest *hongs* (major trading houses or companies), set up shop here, which explains why many of the streets in the district bear its name: Jardine's Bazaar, Jardine's Crescent and Yee Wo St (Cantonese for 'Jardine Matheson'). There is a surfeit of department stores and smaller outlets selling eclectic fashion in the area. Jardine's Bazaar has low-cost garments, and there are several sample shops for cheap jeans in Lee Garden Rd.

## CAUSEWAY BAY

### ◉ SEE
Noonday Gun.....................**1** B2
Tin Hau Temple ...............**2** D2
Victoria Park....................**3** C2

### ▢ SHOP
Camper..............................**4** B2
D-Mop ..............................**5** B2
Dada Cabaret Voltaire.....**6** B3
Island Beverley.................**7** B3
Spy....................................**8** B4

### 🍴 EAT
Arirang .............................**9** B3
Go Sushi.........................**10** B3
Gogo Café ......................**11** C4
Kung Tak Lam.................**12** C3
Opia.................................**13** C3
Orphée.............................**14** B4
Red Pepper.....................**15** B3
Tai Ping Koon.................**16** B3
W's Entrecote.................**17** A4
Wasabisabi.....................**18** B3

Water Margin ................**19** B3
West Villa ......................**20** C4

### 🍸 DRINK
Brecht's Circle ...............**21** C3
Dickens Bar....................**22** B2
Inn Side Out & East End
Brewery..........................**23** B3
Moon Garden Tea
House .............................**24** B4

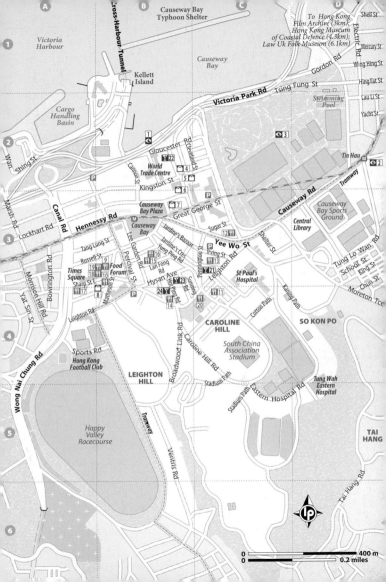

# SEE

## NOONDAY GUN 午炮

**221 Gloucester Rd, Causeway Bay;
subway access 7am-midnight;
M Causeway Bay (exit D1)**

One of the few remnants of Causeway Bay's colonial past is this 3lb quick-firing cannon built by Hotchkiss of Portsmouth in 1901. It's fired daily at noon. Noel Coward made the gun famous with his satirical song 'Mad Dogs and Englishmen' (1924) about colonists who braved the heat of midday while local people stayed indoors: 'In Hong Kong/they strike a gong/and fire off a noonday gun/to reprimand each inmate/who's in late.' The gun stands opposite the Excelsior Hong Kong hotel and is accessible via a tunnel under the road from the World Trade Centre basement, through a door marked 'Car Park Shroff, Marina Club & Noon Gun'.

## TIN HAU TEMPLE 天后廟

**☎ 2721 2326; 10 Tin Hau Temple Rd, Causeway Bay; 7am-6pm; M Tin Hau (exit B)**

Southeast of Victoria Park, Hong Kong Island's most famous Tin Hau temple is small; before reclamation in the last century, this temple, dedicated to the patroness of seafarers, stood on the waterfront.

Victoria Park

## WORTH A TRIP

So-called Island East runs along the island's northern coast and is a large, primarily residential district that has a handful of top-class museums.

**Hong Kong Film Archive** ( ☎ 2739 2139; www.filmarchive.gov.hk; 50 Lei King Rd, Sai Wan Ho; admission free; ☽ 10am-8pm, resource centre 10am-7pm Mon-Wed & Fri, 10am-5pm Sat, 1-5pm Sun; Ⓜ Sai Wan Ho, exit A) This is the place to find out what lies (or perhaps lurks) behind Hong Kong's hard-boiled film industry. The archive houses some 5600 films, runs a rich calendar of local and foreign movie screenings in its 127-seat **cinema** ( ☎ 2734 9009; tickets $30-50; ☽ box office noon-8pm Mon-Wed & Fri-Sun) and exhibits wonderful posters and other fine film paraphernalia. Check the website for screenings and times.

The history of Hong Kong's coastal defence is presented at **Hong Kong Museum of Coastal Defence** ( ☎ 2569 1500; http://hk.history.museum; 175 Tung Hei Rd, Shau Kei Wan; adult/child $10/5, free Wed; ☽ 10am-5pm Fri-Wed; ▣ 84 Ⓜ Shau Kei Wan, exit B2, then 15min walk north along Tung Hei Rd ▣ 85) in restored Lei Yue Mun Fort (1887), which took quite a beating during WWII. Well-presented exhibits in the old redoubt cover the Ming and Qing dynasties, the colonial years, the Japanese invasion and the return of Hong Kong to Chinese sovereignty. There's a historical trail through casements, tunnels and observation posts almost down to the coast.

The small **Law Uk Folk Museum** ( ☎ 2896 7006; http://hk.history.museum; 14 Kut Shing St, Chai Wan; admission free; ☽ 10am-1pm & 2-6pm Mon-Wed, Fri & Sat, 1-6pm Sun; Ⓜ Chai Wan, exit B) is housed in two restored Hakka village houses that have been declared a historical monument. The quiet courtyard and surrounding bamboo groves are peaceful and evocative, and the displays – furniture, household items and farming implements – are simple but charming.

It has been a place of worship for three centuries, though the current structure is only about 200 years old. The central shrine contains a blackened face Tin Hau effigy.

◉ **VICTORIA PARK** NOV 6/08
維多利亞公園
☎ 2570 6186; www.lcsd.gov.hk/parks/vp /en/index.php; Causeway Rd, Causeway Bay; admission free; ☽ 24hr; Ⓜ Causeway Bay (exit E), Tin Hau (exit A2) ▣

Lots of older folks either doing class or "stretching" on their own

At 17 hectares, Victoria Park is one of the biggest patches of public greenery in urban Hong Kong, and a popular city escape. The best time to take a stroll around is during weekday mornings when it becomes a forest of people practising the slow-motion choreography of t'ai chi. The park becomes a vibrant flower market a few days before the Chinese New Year.

## WHAT'S GOING UP & DOWN

A sure sign that a building is going up (or coming down) in Hong Kong is the arrival of truckloads of bamboo poles for scaffolding. The poles are lashed together with plastic bindings to form a grid and the structure is then covered in green netting. It may not look very high-tech, but bamboo is lighter, cheaper and more flexible than the bolted steel tubing used by scaffolders in the West. It also copes much better with tensile stress, as you'll see if you watch builders scuttle around in their thin-soled slippers, barely causing a ripple.

# 🛍 SHOP

Causeway Bay is a crush of department stores and smaller outlets selling eclectic fashion. Jardine's Bazaar has low-cost garments, and there are several sample shops for cheap jeans in Lee Garden Rd.

## 📷 CAMPER
*Clothing & Accessories*

☎ 2882 9310; 2 Kingston St, Causeway Bay; ☻ noon-10pm; Ⓜ Causeway Bay
Camper, emblazoned with thought-provoking slogans and aphorisms out front, is one of the most popular outlets in Hong Kong for locally designed fashion.

## 📷 D-MOP
*Clothing & Accessories*

☎ 2203 4130; www.d-mop.com; Shop B, ground fl, Greenfield Mansion, 8 Kingston St, Causeway Bay; ☻ noon-10pm; Ⓜ Causeway Bay
This is the main outlet for one of Hong Kong's edgier designer lines. Most Cantopop (p188) appears to favour this line.

## 📷 DADA CABARET VOLTAIRE
*Clothing & Accessories*

☎ 2890 1708; Shop F-13A, 1st fl, Fashion Island, 19 Great George St, Causeway Bay; ☻ noon-10pm; Ⓜ Causeway Bay
Sells ragged rainbow colours that are also sported by the staff. This is just one of many fine shops in the Fashion Island micro mall complex.

## 📷 ISLAND BEVERLEY
金百利商場 *Clothing & Accessories*

1 Great George St, Causeway Bay; Ⓜ Causeway Bay
Crammed into buildings, up escalators and in back lanes are Hong Kong's malls of micro-shops selling designer threads, a kaleidoscope of kooky accessories and an Imelda Marcos of funky footwear. Island Beverley is where Hong Kong's youngest mall-trawlers shop for clothes and trinkets and capture their moment of retail therapy on sticker machines.

## SHOCK OF THE NEW

When Hong Kong's trams first started running more than a century ago, they caused a sensation. Stops were packed with people but not many of them actually wanted to go anywhere; a great number just jumped on, walked through having a gawp and treading on toes, then got off again, not quite ready to ride. The trams were also delayed by hawkers who took advantage of the tramway by dragging their heavy carts along the well-made tracks. In 1911, a law was passed banning carts with the same wheel gauge as the trams. The law is still in effect today.

### SPY *Clothing & Accessories*
☎ 2893 7799; www.spyhenrylau.com; Shop C, ground fl, 11 Sharp St East, Causeway Bay; ⏰ 1-11pm; Ⓜ Causeway Bay
Tame yet trendy everyday wear such as slacks and short-sleeve shirts from designer Henry Lau.

# 🍴 EAT

### 🍴 ARIRANG 阿里朗 *Korean* $$
☎ 2506 3298; Shop 1105, 11th fl, Food Forum, Times Sq, 1 Matheson St, Causeway Bay; ⏰ noon-3pm & 6-11pm; Ⓜ Causeway Bay
A branch of the upmarket restaurant chain with usual barbecues along with excellent hotpot dishes. It's great for a bargain set-lunch.

### 🍴 GO SUSHI
元綠壽司 *Japanese* $
☎ 2803 5909; 3 Matheson St, Causeway Bay; ⏰ 11.30am-4am; Ⓜ Causeway Bay
Go Sushi is Hong Kong's most exotic fast-food chain. The sushi tears around on a conveyor belt and is reasonably fresh. The only drawback is the potentially long wait for seats, especially during the manic lunch hour (1pm to 2pm). It's a great place for a late snack though.

### 🍴 GOGO CAFÉ *not there anymore!*
*International, Fusion* $$
☎ 2881 5598; 11 Caroline Hill Rd, Causeway Bay; ⏰ noon-10pm Mon-Sat; Ⓜ Causeway Bay
East meets West for spaghetti with *mentaiko* (fish roe) or linguine with Chinese clams and bacon at this gentle little café-restaurant. The theme here is part Japanese teahouse, part cool café, and the light meals and home-made desserts (!) make Gogo a good place to re-energise between lunch and dinner.

### 🍴 KUNG TAK LAM 功德林
*Vegetarian Chinese* $$
☎ 2881 9966; ground fl, Lok Sing Centre, 31 Yee Wo St, Causeway Bay; ⏰ 11am-11pm; Ⓜ Causeway Bay
This long-established place, which serves Shanghai-style meatless dishes, is more modern-feeling

than most vegetarian eateries in Hong Kong. All veggies served here are 100% organic and dishes are free of MSG.

### 🍴 OPIA

*International, Fusion* $$$$

☎ 3196 9100; Jia Hotel, 1-5 Irving St, Causeway Bay; ⏰ noon-3pm Mon-Fri, 6-11pm Mon-Sat; Ⓜ Causeway Bay

This super-stylish restaurant (think lush colours and rich textures) in the Starck-designed Jia Hotel serves 'Australian freestyle' cuisine and has gobbled up a remarkable number of awards in a very short time. Not every dish works, but most (and the décor) certainly do.

### 🍴 ORPHÉE *French* $$$

☎ 2577 3111; www.orphee.com.hk; 1 Hoi Ping Rd, Causeway Bay; ⏰ noon-3pm & 7pm-midnight; Ⓜ Causeway Bay

This minimalist but cosy restaurant really is a small pocket of Paris in Causeway Bay. If you feel like a fix of foie gras, this is your choice.

### 🍴 RED PEPPER

南北樓 *Sichuanese* $$

☎ 2577 3811; 7 Lan Fong Rd, Causeway Bay; ⏰ 11.30am-midnight; Ⓜ Causeway Bay

If you want to set your palate alight, try this friendly, long-

established eatery's sliced pork in chilli sauce, accompanied by *dan dan min* (noodles in a spicy peanut broth). Also recommended are the deep-fried beans and sizzling prawns.

### 🍴 TAI PING KOON

太平館餐廳
*International, Chinese* $$$

☎ 2576 9161; 6 Pak Sha Rd, Causeway Bay; ⏰ 11am-midnight; Ⓜ Causeway Bay

This place has been around since 1860 and offers an incredible mix of Western and Chinese flavours – what Hong Kong people called 'soy sauce restaurants' in pre-fusion days. Try the borscht and the smoked pomfret or some roast pigeon, all specialities of the house.

### 🍴 WASABISABI

*Japanese* $$$

*[handwritten: Nov 7/08 Great service + ambience]*

☎ 2506 0009; Shop 1301, 13th fl, Food Forum, Times Square, 1 Matheson St, Causeway Bay; ⏰ noon-3pm daily, 6pm-midnight Sun-Thu, 6pm-2am Fri & Sat; Ⓜ Causeway Bay

Excellent Japanese cuisine, impeccable service and an over-the-top interior. From cable vines through to lipstick-reds and into the sweeping sushi bar of palm leaves and ostrich feathers, this is eclectic magnificence. The bar turns into a club at night.

*Felt like dim sum in chinese Yorkville!*

*NOV 7/08*

## 🍴 WATER MARGIN
### 梁山泊 *Northern Chinese* $$$
☎ 3102 0088; Shop 1205, 12th fl, Food Forum, Times Square, 1 Matheson St, Causeway Bay; 🕐 noon-3pm & 6-11pm; Ⓜ Causeway Bay

Art is imitating life again, this time at this mock-up of a market in Shandong Province. The dining room looks like it's been kitted out with Chinese antiques from Hollywood Rd but the food, service and attitude is definitely of this century. A pleasure.

## 🍴 WEST VILLA
### 西苑酒家 *Cantonese* $$$
☎ 2882 2110; Shop 101-102, 1st fl, Lee Gardens Two, 28 Yun Ping Rd, Causeway Bay; 🕐 11am-11.30pm; Ⓜ Causeway Bay

When we die and go to Cantonese heaven, this place is going to be doing the catering. Everything is superb here but start with the celebrated (and incomparable) *cha siu fan* (barbecued pork with rice) and try the pigeon and crab dishes. *Best we've had!*

Red Pepper restaurant

# >HONG KONG ISLAND: ISLAND SOUTH

Though largely residential, the Southern District, encompassing everything from Big Wave Bay and Shek O in the east to Aberdeen and Ap Lei Chau in the west, is full of attractions and things to do. Indeed, at times it can almost feel like Hong Kong Island's backyard playground – from the beaches of Repulse Bay and Deep Water Bay and the outdoor activities available at Shek O, to Stanley Market (a shoppers' paradise) and Ocean Park near Aberdeen (still the largest amusement and theme park in the territory even after the advent of Hong Kong Disneyland). And one of Hong Kong's most enjoyable long-range walks, the 78km Wilson Trail, starts just north of Stanley. In general, the best way to get around this part of Hong Kong Island is by bus but an extension of the MTR's Island line is planned, which would bring rail transport to the southern part of Hong Kong Island.

## ISLAND SOUTH

### ◉ SEE
Hong Kong Maritime
Museum ..................... (see 2)
Kwun Yam Shrine ............ 1 C2
Longevity Bridge......... (see 1)
Murray House.................. 2 D1
Ocean Park ..................... 3 B4

Repulse Bay...................... 4 C2
Repulse Bay................. (See 9)

### 🛍 SHOP
Stanley Market............... 5 D1

### 🍴 EAT
Boathouse ...................... 6 D1
Lucy's............................... 7 D1
Top Deck at the Jumbo.... 8 B4
Verandah ......................... 9 B2

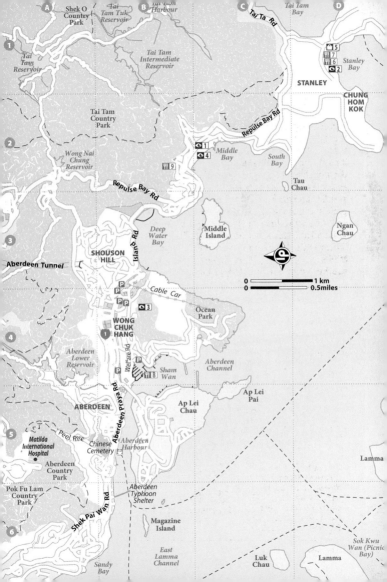

# 👁 SEE

## 👁 HONG KONG MARITIME MUSEUM
香港海事博物館

☎ 2813 2322; www.hkmaritime museum.org; ground fl, Murray House, Stanley Plaza, Stanley; adult/child $20/10; ⏱ 10am-6pm Tue-Fri & Sun, 10am-7pm Sat; 🚌 6, 6A, 6X, 260

Hong Kong's long-awaited museum, dedicated to what put it on the map in the first place, has finally opened in Stanley's Murray House (below). It's not huge – everything is contained in two rooms (Ancient and Modern Galleries) – but there are some wonderful mock-ups of Tang dynasty seagoing vessels, a nice collection of trade art (including sketches by George Chinnery) and a fair amount of hands-on exhibits, including a simulator that allows you to sit on the bridge of a container ship and guide it (maybe) into Victoria Harbour.

## 👁 OCEAN PARK
香港海洋公園

☎ 2552 0291; www.oceanpark.com.hk; Ocean Park Rd, Aberdeen; adult/child $185/93; ⏱ 10am-6pm; 🚌 6X, 73, 629 (Ocean Park Citybus), green minibus 6

Hong Kong's biggest home-grown theme park, with roller coasters, the world's largest aquarium and an atoll, both amuses and educates. The two-part complex is linked by a scenic (slightly hair-raising) cable-car ride. The park entrance is on the lowland side southeast of Aberdeen and the main section is on the headlands, with terrific views of the South China Sea.

## 👁 REPULSE BAY 淺水灣
🚌 6, 6A, 6X or 260

Though it can get packed at the weekend, and even during the week in summer, the long beach at Repulse Bay is a good place if you like people-watching. At its southeastern end is an unusual shrine to **Kwun Yam**, the God of Mercy. The surrounding area has

---

### IT'S A CHINESE PUZZLE

When the Hong Kong government pulled down Hong Kong's oldest colonial building in 1982 to make room for the new Bank of China, it promised to rebuild **Murray House** elsewhere at a later date. The time finally came in the mid-1990s and the place chosen was Stanley – but the pieces had been so badly numbered and catalogued that it took workers 3½ years to put this colossal puzzle back together again. And, when they'd finished, they didn't know what to do with six extra columns. You'll see them standing idly to the left along the waterfront promenade.

---

Ocean Park cable cars

an amazing assembly of mosaics, deities and figures – goldfish, rams, statues of Tin Hau and other southern Chinese icons. In front of the shrine, to the left as you face the sea, is **Longevity Bridge**; crossing it is supposed to add three days to your life.

# SHOP

## STANLEY MARKET
赤柱市集

**Stanley Village Rd, Stanley;** ⏰ **9am-6pm;** 🚌 **6, 6A, 6X, 260**
No big bargains nor big stings, just reasonably priced casual clothes (plenty of large sizes), linens, hats, bric-a-brac, toys and formulaic art, all in a nicely confusing maze of alleys running

### HOLE IN THE SOUL
Repulse Bay is home to some of Hong Kong's richest residents, and the hills around the beach are strewn with luxury apartment blocks. Among them is a giant pink, blue and yellow wavy structure with a giant square hole in the middle called the **Repulse Bay**. Apparently this design feature was added on the advice of a feng shui expert.

NEIGHBOURHOODS

ISLAND SOUTH

down to Stanley Bay. It's best to go during the week if possible.

# 🍴 EAT

## 🍴 BOATHOUSE
*International* $$$

☎ 2813 4467; 88 Stanley Main St, Stanley; ☽ noon-midnight Sun-Thu, 11am-1am Fri & Sat, 9am-midnight Sun; 🚌 6, 6A, 6X or 260

All aboard for nautical overload. Salads, bruschetta and Med-inspired mains make up the bulk

of the fleet. Aim for sea views to go with your seafood on this casual yacht house .

## 🍴 LUCY'S
*International* $$$

☎ 2813 9055; 64 Stanley Main St, Stanley; ☽ noon-3pm & 7-10pm Mon-Fri, noon-4pm & 6.30-9.30pm Sat & Sun; 🚌 6, 6A, 6X, 260

This very relaxed place doesn't overwhelm with choice but with quality. The menu changes frequently as fresh produce and

Jumbo Kingdom floating restaurant

inspiration arrive, but the offerings tend toward honest fusion rather than flimflammery. There's a good selection of wines by the glass.

## 🍴 TOP DECK AT THE JUMBO
*Chinese*  $$$

☎ 2552 3331; www.cafédecogroup.com; Jumbo Kingdom, Shum Wan Pier Dr, Wong Chuk Hang, Aberdeen; ⏰ 11.30am-midnight Tue-Thu & Sun, 11.30am-1am Fri & Sat; 🚌 70, 73, 973

This new spin on a Hong Kong institution sits atop the Jumbo Kingdom, the larger of two floating restaurants moored in Aberdeen Harbour. But while the restaurant below offers lacklustre seafood and a 'Beijing's Imperial Palace meets Las Vegas casino' décor, the Top Deck promises grown-up food and surrounds. The Sunday unlimited seafood and champagne buffet (adult/child $328/198, 11.30am to 4.30pm) is a great splurge. There's

free transport for diners from the pier on Aberdeen Promenade.

## 🍴 VERANDAH
*International, Asian*  $$$$

☎ 2292 2822; 1st fl, The Repulse Bay, 109 Repulse Bay Rd, Repulse Bay ⏰ breakfast 7-10am Mon-Sat, 7-10.30am Sun, brunch & lunch noon-3pm, afternoon tea 3-5.30pm, dinner 6.30-11pm; 🚌 6, 6A, 6X, 260

This place is housed in a replicated colonial structure in front of the wavy Repulse Bay condos (p107), which is meant to recall the stunning Repulse Bay Hotel that was bulldozed in 1982. Wooden ceiling fans swooshing away, palms in their pots and a sea-facing outlook all lend a tropical feel. The Verandah is hushed and formal with heavy white tablecloths and demurely clinking cutlery. The brunch is famous (book well ahead), and the afternoon tea is the south side's best.

# >KOWLOON: TSIM SHA TSUI & TSIM SHA TSUI EAST

Tsim Sha Tsui (Sharp Sandy Point; roughly pronounced chim-sa-choy) is Hong Kong's tourist ghetto. Countless clothing and shoe shops, restaurants, pubs, sleazy bars, camera and electronics stores, and hotels are somehow crammed into an area not much bigger than 1 sq km. Around Ashley, Hankow and Lock Rds is a warren of shops, restaurants and bars. It's a fun area to wander around, particularly in the evening. To the east is the reclaimed (and rather soulless) area of Tsim Sha Tsui East, awash with top-end hotels and world-class museums. But more than anything else Tsim

# TSIM SHA TSUI & TSIM SHA TSUI EAST

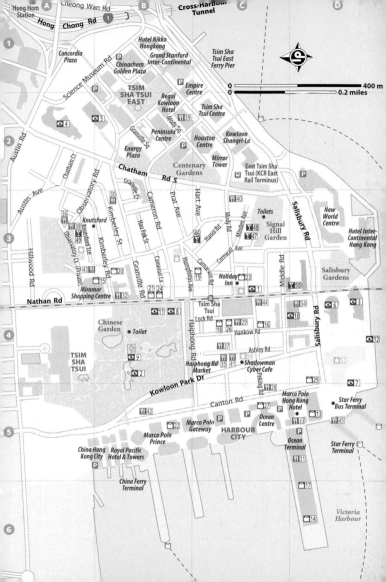

Sha Tsui is about shopping. But beware: Nathan Rd, the main tourist strip here, is one of the very few places where you'll find merchants poised to rip you off, especially when buying electronic goods or photographic equipment. The best hunting grounds for clothing warehouse sales and factory extras in Tsim Sha Tsui are generally at the eastern end of Granville Rd. Also check out nearby Austin Ave and Chatham Rd South.

# 👁 SEE

## ◉ CHUNGKING MANSIONS 重慶大廈

☎ 36-44 Nathan Rd, Tsim Sha Tsui; Ⓜ Tsim Sha Tsui (exit D1)

Say 'budget accommodation' and 'Hong Kong' in one breath and everyone thinks of Chungking Mansions, a place like no other in the world. This huge, ramshackle high-rise dump in the heart of Tsim Sha Tsui caters to virtually all needs – from finding a bed and a curry lunch to changing your Burmese kyat and getting your hair cut – but you may be put off by the undercurrent of sleaze and the peculiar odour of cooking fat, incense and sewage. The building's infamy is fuelled by tales both tall and true of conflagrations, crimes and unclaimed bodies; everyone should come here once. The entrance to Chungking Mansions is via Chungking Arcade, a parade of shops that faces Nathan Rd.

## ◉ HONG KONG MUSEUM OF ART 香港藝術博物館

☎ 2721 0116; http://hk.art.museum; 10 Salisbury Rd, Tsim Sha Tsui; adult/

child $10/5, free Wed; 🕙 10am-6pm Sun-Fri, 10am-8pm Sat; Ⓜ Tsim Sha Tsui (exit E) 🚢 Star Ferry (Tsim Sha Tsui)

This museum does a credible job of showing classical Chinese art, paintings and lithographs of old Hong Kong and (mostly) calligraphy in the Xubaizhi collection in a total of seven galleries spread over six floors. There are worthwhile international exhibitions, but the gallery falls short on contemporary art, especially of the local variety.

## ◉ HONG KONG MUSEUM OF HISTORY 香港歷史博物館

☎ 2724 9042; http://hk.history.museum; 100 Chatham Rd S, Tsim Sha Tsui East; adult/child $10/5, free Wed; 🕙 10am-6pm Mon & Wed-Sat, 10am-7pm Sun; Ⓜ Tsim Sha Tsui (exit A2) 🚌 5, 8

Hong Kong's best museum focuses on the territory's archaeology, natural history, ethnography and local history. It is well worth a visit to understand how Hong Kong presents its history to itself and the world (above). This can be in the form of video programmes. Free guided tours of the museum are available in English at 10.30am and 2.30pm on Saturday and Sunday.

## CULTURAL KALEIDOSCOPE

One of the HKTB's more interesting offerings by the **Hong Kong Tourist Board** (HKTB; ☎ 2508 1234; www .discoverhongkong.com) is a series of a dozen free cultural programs in English called 'Meet the People' and run by local experts in their fields. Topics covered include antiques, architecture, Cantonese opera, Chinese medicine, Chinese cake-making, Chinese tea, diamonds, feng shui, kung fu, jade and pearl shopping, t'ai chi.

## ◉ HONG KONG SCIENCE MUSEUM 香港科學館

☎ 2732 3232; http://hk.science .museum; 2 Science Museum Rd, Tsim Sha Tsui East; adult/child $25/12.50, free Wed; ⏱ 1-9pm Mon-Wed & Fri, 10am-9pm Sat & Sun; Ⓜ Tsim Sha Tsui (exit A2) 🚍 5, 5C, 8

The Hong Kong Science Museum is a multilevel complex with more than 500 displays on computers, energy, physics, robotics, telecommunications, health and various other subjects in 18 galleries. Although some of the exhibits are beginning to look a little dated, the numerous buttons to push and robot arms to operate – especially on the mammoth Energy Machine – will keep young (and some older) visitors entertained.

## ◉ HONG KONG SPACE MUSEUM 香港太空館

☎ 2721 0226; http://hk.space .museum; 10 Salisbury Rd, Tsim Sha Tsui; adult/child $10/5, free Wed; ⏱ 1-9pm Mon & Wed-Fri, 10am-9pm Sat & Sun; Ⓜ Tsim Sha Tsui (exit E) 🚢 Star Ferry (Tsim Sha Tsui)

Just east of the Kowloon Cultural Centre, this golf ball–shaped building consists of the Hall of Space Science on the ground floor and the Hall of Astronomy and Stanley Ho Space Theatre planetarium on the 1st floor. Exhibits include a lump of moon rock, rocket-ship models and NASA's 1962 *Mercury* space capsule and you can experience a simulated moon walk. The space theatre screens 'sky shows' and Omnimax films (adult/child $32/16 stalls, $24/12 front stalls, first show 1.30pm Monday to Friday, 12.20pm Saturday, 11.10am Sunday) mostly in Cantonese, with translations by headphones.

## ◉ KCR CLOCK TOWER 尖沙咀前九廣鐵路鐘樓

Tsim Sha Tsui Public Pier, Salisbury Rd, Tsim Sha Tsui; Ⓜ Tsim Sha Tsui (exit E) 🚢 Star Ferry (Tsim Sha Tsui)

This 44m-high clock tower, built in 1915, is all that remains of the southern terminus of the Kowloon-Canton Railway (KCR), inaugurated in 1916 and torn down in 1978. The original colonial building was too small to handle the large volume of passenger traffic and operations moved to the modern station at Hung Hom.

### ◉ KOWLOON MOSQUE & ISLAMIC CENTRE 九龍清真寺

☎ 2724 0095; 105 Nathan Rd, Tsim Sha Tsui; admission free; ⏰ 5am-10pm; Ⓜ Tsim Sha Tsui (exit A1)

Hong Kong's largest mosque, completed in 1984, occupies the site of a previous mosque built in 1896 for Muslim Indian troops garrisoned in barracks at what is now known as Kowloon Park. The mosque has a handsome dome, minarets and a carved marble exterior. It is capable of accommodating 7000 worshippers. Muslims are welcome to attend services at the mosque but non-Muslims should ask permission to enter. Remember to remove your shoes before entering.

Tsim Sha Tsui promenade and Hong Kong harbour

## KOWLOON PARK
### 九龍公園

☎ 2724 3344; www.lcsd.gov.hk/parks /kp/en/index.php; 22 Austin Rd, Tsim Sha Tsui; admission free; ⏰ 6am-midnight; Ⓜ Tsim Sha Tsui (exit A1), Jordan (exit C1)

Built on the site of a barracks for Indian soldiers in the colonial army, Kowloon Park is an oasis of greenery and a refreshing escape from the hustle and bustle of Tsim Sha Tsui. Pathways and walls crisscross the grass, birds hop around in cages, and towers and viewpoints dot the landscape. The **Sculpture Walk** features works by local and international sculptors. The new **Hong Kong Heritage Discovery Centre** ( ☎ 2208 4400; www .amo.gov.hk; admission free; ⏰ 10am-6pm Mon-Sat, 10am-7pm Sun) of the Antiquities and Monuments Office is located in the former Whitfield Barracks (1910) in the parks southwestern corner and focuses on Hong Kong's architectural heritage.

## PENINSULA HOTEL HONG KONG 香港半島酒店

☎ 2920 2888; www.peninsula.com; cnr Salisbury & Nathan Rds, Tsim Sha Tsui; Ⓜ Tsim Sha Tsui (exit E)

More than a Hong Kong landmark, the Peninsula, in the throne-like building opposite the Hong Kong Space Museum, is one of the world's great hotels. Land reclamation has robbed the hotel of its top waterfront location, but the breathtaking lobby of the original building is well worth a visit. And it's by far the classiest place in town to take tea (left).

## TSIM SHA TSUI PROMENADE
### 尖沙咀海濱長廊 ~NOV 6 ~ romantic walk!

South of Salisbury Rd along Victoria Harbour, Tsim Sha Tsui; admission free; 🚢 Star Ferry (Tsim Sha Tsui pier), hydrofoil (Tsim Sha Tsui East pier)

Stretching along what is arguably the most dramatic harbour in the world, this open-air walkway offers superb views of Hong Kong Island. Along the first part of the promenade the **Avenue of the Stars** pays homage to the Hong Kong film industry and its stars, with handprints, sculptures and information boards. The promenade is

---

### A VERY CLOSE SHAVE

Among the oft-told tales about the hotel affectionately known as 'the Pen' is the one about the spy with the razor. After the capitulation of British forces in Hong Kong to the Japanese on Christmas Day 1941, it was learned that the manager of the hotel barbershop had been a Japanese spy (and naval commander to boot), taking advantage of the chatty, informal atmosphere of the surrounds to collect useful information about the troop movements and so on.

---

TSIM SHA TSUI & TSIM SHA TSUI EAST

a lovely place to stroll during the day, but it's best at night when the **Symphony of Lights**, a spectacular sound-and-light show involving more than 33 buildings (21 of them on the Hong Kong Island skyline), which takes place from 8pm to 8.20pm daily. *overrated!*

# SHOP

### CHINESE ARTS & CRAFTS
中藝 *Gifts & Souvenirs*
☎ 2735 4061; www.crcretail.com; 1st fl, Star House, 3 Salisbury Rd, Tsim Sha Tsui; ☽ 10am-9.30pm; Ⓜ Tsim Sha Tsui ⛴ Star Ferry (Tsim Sha Tsui)
This Aladdin's department store of high-end gifts and souvenirs is probably the best place to buy quality bric-a-brac and other Chinese *chotchkies* (cheap, flashy trinkets).

### GIGA SPORTS *Outdoor Gear*
☎ 2115 9930; Shop 244-247, 2nd fl, Ocean Terminal, Harbour City, Canton Rd, Tsim Sha Tsui; ☽ 10.30am-9pm; Ⓜ Tsim Sha Tsui ⛴ Star Ferry (Tsim Sha Tsui)
This large shop has a wide range of sports equipment, backpacks, clothing and footwear.

### I.T *Clothing & Accessories*
☎ 2736 9152; Shop 1030, 1st fl, Miramar Shopping Centre, 1-23 Kimberley Rd, Tsim Sha Tsui; ☽ noon-10pm; Ⓜ Tsim Sha Tsui

This shop and the women's-only **b+ab** shop next door both sell the cute, trendy gear that can be found everywhere in Hong Kong. There are i.t shops in all the major shopping areas.

### KS AHLUWALIA & SONS
*Sporting Goods*
☎ 2368 8334; 8C Hankow Rd, Tsim Sha Tsui; ☽ 10am-7.30pm Mon-Sat, 10am-5pm Sun; Ⓜ Tsim Sha Tsui
This family-run store is well stocked with golf gear, tennis racquets, cricket bats, shirts and balls. Staff know their stock well.

### LANE CRAWFORD
連卡佛 *Department Store*
☎ 2118 3428; www.lanecrawford.com; ground & 1st fl, Ocean Terminal, Harbour City, Salisbury Rd; ☽ 10am-9pm; Ⓜ Tsim Sha Tsui ⛴ Star Ferry (Tsim Sha Tsui)
Hong Kong's first (and most successful) Western-style department store is still a very upmarket place – a sort of local response to Harvey Nichols in London.

### OCEAN SKY DIVERS
海天潛水訓練中心
*Sporting Goods*
☎ 2366 3738; www.oceanskydiver .com; 1st fl, 17-19 Lock Rd, Tsim Sha Tsui; ☽ 10.30am-9pm; Ⓜ Tsim Sha Tsui
This shop, despite its somewhat ambiguous name, has the whole

---

## SHOPPING ON THE DEFENCE

Most shops are loath to give refunds but they can usually be persuaded to exchange purchases that can be resold; just make sure you get a receipt. When buying electronic goods, always beware of merchandise imported by an unauthorised agent, as this may void your warranty. If you have any trouble with dodgy merchants, contact HKTB's **Quality Tourism Services** (QTS; ☎ 2508 1234; www.qtshk.com) – and they are members of that association. (The QTS logo should be displayed on the front door; at last count there were upwards of 6000 members.) Otherwise, call the **Hong Kong Consumer Council** ( ☎ 2929 2222; www.consumer.org.hk).

---

range of diving and snorkelling gear – but no parachutes.

### OM INTERNATIONAL
*Jewellery*
☎ 2366 3421; www.omperals.com; Ste A3, 1st fl, Friend's House, 6 Carnarvon Rd, Tsim Sha Tsui; ⏰ 9.30am-6pm Mon-Sat; Ⓜ Tsim Sha Tsui
An excellent selection of saltwater and freshwater pearls awaits you here and there's a lot more on of-fer than what you see. The staff are friendly, helpful and very honest.

### ONESTO PHOTO COMPANY 忠誠
*Photographic Equipment*
☎ 2723 4668; Shop 18, Block B, ground fl, Champagne Ct, 16 Kimberley Rd, Tsim Sha Tsui; ⏰ 10.30am-8.30pm Mon-Sat, 11am-7pm Sun; Ⓜ Tsim Sha Tsui
This retail outlet, which stocks mostly film cameras, has price tags on its equipment (a rarity in Tsim Sha Tsui) but there's always a bit of latitude for bargaining.

### OPAL MINE
澳之寶有限公司 *Jewellery*
☎ 2721 9933; www.opalnet.com; Shop G & H, ground fl, Burlington Arcade, 92-94 Nathan Rd, Tsim Sha Tsui; ⏰ 9.30am-7pm; Ⓜ Tsim Sha Tsui
More of a museum than a shop, this place lives up to its name with a truly vast selection of Australian opals that makes for fascinating viewing and buying, should you be so tempted.

### PAGE ONE *Books*
☎ 2730 6080; www.pageonegroup .com; Shop 3202, 3rd fl, Gateway Arcade, Harbour City, Canton Rd, Tsim Sha Tsui; ⏰ 10.30am-10pm Mon-Thu, 10.30am-10.30pm Fri-Sun; Ⓜ Tsim Sha Tsui ⚓ Star Ferry (Tsim Sha Tsui)
A chain, yes, but one with at-titude. Page One has Hong Kong's best selection of art and design magazines and books, and it's also strong on photography, literature, film and children's books.

## ☐ PREMIER JEWELLERY
### 愛寶珠寶 *Jewellery*
☎ 2368 0003; Shop G14-15, ground fl, Holiday Inn Golden Mile Shopping Mall, 50 Nathan Rd, Tsim Sha Tsui; 🕙 10am-7.30pm Mon-Sat, 10.30am-4pm Sun; Ⓜ Tsim Sha Tsui

This family business is directed by a qualified gemologist and is one of our favourite shops. If you're looking for something in particular, give them a day's notice to have a selection ready for your arrival. They can also help you design your own piece.

## ☐ SAM'S TAILOR
### *Clothing & Accessories*
☎ 2367 9423, 2367 0363; Shop K, ground fl, Burlington Arcade, 92-94 Nathan Rd, Tsim Sha Tsui; 🕙 10am-7.30pm Mon-Sat, 10am-noon Sun; Ⓜ Tsim Sha Tsui

Sam's may not the best tailor in Hong Kong, but it's the most aggressively marketed. Sam's has stitched up everyone – from royally and rock stars to mere mortals like us. The turnaround on most items is two or three days, including two fittings.

Aqua restaurant & city views

## ⚙ STAR COMPUTER CITY
星光電腦城 *Computers*

☎ 2736 2608; 2nd fl, Star House, 3 Salisbury Rd, Tsim Sha Tsui; ⏰ 10am or 10.30am-7.30pm or 8pm; Ⓜ Tsim Sha Tsui 🚢 Star Ferry (Tsim Sha Tsui)

This is largest complex of computer outlets in Tsim Sha Tsui, with some two dozen shops. Check out **Reptron** ( ☎ 2730 2891; Shop B2, 2nd fl) for desktops, laptops and PDAs, and **2C** ( ☎ 2375 2375; Shop A4-6, 2nd fl) for accessories such as modem protectors, adaptors and cables.

## 📕 SWINDON BOOKS
辰衝 *Books*

☎ 2366 8001; www.swindonbooks.com; 13-15 Lock Rd, Tsim Sha Tsui; ⏰ 9am-6.30pm Mon-Thu, 9am-7.30pm Fri & Sat, 12.30-6.30pm Sun; Ⓜ Tsim Sha Tsui

This is one of the best 'real' (as opposed to 'supermarket') bookshops. Its sister store is Central's Hong Kong Book Centre (p51).

## 🛍 WWW.IZZUE.COM
*Clothing & Accessories*

☎ 2992 0631; www.izzue.com; Shop 2225, 2nd fl, Gateway Arcade, Harbour City, Canton Rd, Tsim Sha Tsui; ⏰ 11am-9pm; Ⓜ Tsim Sha Tsui 🚢 Star Ferry (Tsim Sha Tsui)

You'll find simple, energetic and comfortable styles in this chain of super-groovy boutiques. There are almost two dozen outlets throughout the territory.

## SHIPPING NEWS

Goods can be mailed home by post, and some shops will package and post the goods for you. It's a good idea to find out whether you will have to clear the goods through customs at the other end. If the goods are fragile, it is sensible to buy 'all risks' insurance. Smaller items can be shipped from the post office. **United Parcel Service** (UPS; ☎ 2735 3535) also offers services from Hong Kong to some 200 destinations. **DHL Express** ( ☎ 2400 3388), with outlets in many MTR stations, is another option.

## 🍴 EAT

## 🍴 AQUA *Italian, Japanese* $$$$

☎ 3427 2288; 29th fl, One Peking, 1 Peking Rd; ⏰ noon-11.30pm; Ⓜ Tsim Sha Tsui

This ultra-minimalist place, just below a fabulous bar called Aqua Spirit, has a split personality, made up of Aqua Roma and Aqua Tokyo. The food is good but the views are simply astonishing.

## 🍴 BRANTO PURE VEGETARIAN INDIAN FOOD
*Vegetarian Indian* $

☎ 2366 8171; 1st fl, 9 Lock Rd; ⏰ 11am-3pm & 6-11pm; Ⓜ Tsim Sha Tsui

Head to this excellent Indian club if you want to try South Indian dishes. Order a *thali* – a steel tray

NEIGHBOURHOODS

TSIM SHA TSUI & TSIM SHA TSUI EAST

of *idlis* (soft rice cakes) and *dosas* with dipping sauces.

### CHANG WON KOREAN RESTAURANT
莊園韓國料理 *Korean* $$

☎ 2368 4606; 1G Kimberley St;
🕑 11.30am-midnight; Ⓜ Tsim Sha Tsui
If you're looking for really au-thentic Korean food – barbecues with all the *kimchi* (spicy pickled cabbage) you can manage – head for this place, just one of several restaurants along a stretch that makes up Tsim Sha Tsui's 'Little Korea'.

### DAN RYAN'S CHICAGO GRILL *American* $$$

☎ 2735 6111; Shop 315, 3rd fl, Ocean Terminal, Harbour City, Canton Rd, Tsim Sha Tsui; 🕑 11am-midnight Mon-Fri, 10am-midnight Sat & Sun; Ⓜ Tsim Sha Tsui 🚢 Star Ferry (Tsim Sha Tsui)
The theme at Dan Ryan's is 'Chica-go', including a model elevated rail system overhead and jazz and big-band music on the sound system. It is also one of the best places for burgers and ribs (half/full rack $132/198) in Hong Kong.

### DONG 東宮 *Cantonese* $$$

☎ 2315 5166; Arcade Level 2, Miramar Hotel, 118-130 Nathan Rd, Tsim Sha Tsui; 🕑 11.30am-2.30pm Mon-Fri, 10.30am-3.30pm Sun, 6.30-10.30pm daily; Ⓜ Tsim Sha Tsui

It's the classic hotel restaurant interior right down to the Muzak, but the menu at 'East' does offer adventurous Cantonese dishes, including seafood soups and a forest of fungus.

### EASTERN PALACE CHIU CHOW RESTAURANT
東鑾閣潮州酒家
*Chiu Chow* $$$

☎ 2730 6011; Shop 308, 3rd fl, Marco Polo Hong Kong Hotel, 3 Canton Rd, Tsim Sha Tsui; 🕑 10.30am-10.30pm; Ⓜ Tsim Sha Tsui
Some of the best Chiu Chow–style dim sum is served at this large hotel restaurant from 11am to 4pm daily.

### FAT ANGELO'S
*Italian-American* $$$

☎ 2730 4788; 8 Minden Ave, Tsim Sha Tsui; 🕑 noon-midnight; Ⓜ Tsim Sha Tsui
Huge portions, free salads, unlimited bread and relatively low prices are the keys to success at this chain of Italian-American restaurants.

### FELIX
*International, Fusion* $$$$

☎ 2315 3188; 28th fl, Peninsula Hotel Hong Kong, Salisbury Rd, Tsim Sha Tsui; 🕑 6pm-10.30am; Ⓜ Tsim Sha Tsui 🚢 Star Ferry (Tsim Sha Tsui)
Felix has a fantastic setting, both inside and out. You're sure to pay

as much attention to the views and the Philippe Starck–designed interior as the fusion food (think dishes such as lobster nachos, Hoisin grilled ribs). Towering ceilings and copper-clad columns surround the Art Deco tables, while the design of and view from the men's room is almost beyond belief.

### ♙ GAYLORD 爵樂印度餐廳
*Indian* $$

☎ 2376 1001; 1st fl, Ashley Centre, 23-25 Ashley Rd, Tsim Sha Tsui; ⏱ noon-3pm & 6-11pm; M Tsim Sha Tsui
The dim lighting and live Indian music set the scene for enjoying the excellent *rogan josh, dhal* and other favourite dishes at Hong Kong's oldest Indian restaurant, which has been operating since 1972. There are lots of vegetarian choices as well.

### ♙ HUTONG 胡同
*Northern Chinese* $$$$

☎ 3428 8342; 28th fl, One Peking, 1 Peking Rd; ⏱ noon-3pm & 6pm-midnight; M Tsim Sha Tsui ⛴ Star Ferry (Tsim Sha Tsui)
This very stylish Northern Chinese restaurant just below the Aqua (p119) twins is the best of both worlds: old style furnishings and service, and modern food presentation and views. An award-winning stunner.

### ♙ INDONESIAN RESTAURANT 1968 印尼餐廳 *Indonesian* $$

☎ 2619 1926; 2-4A Observatory Ct, Tsim Sha Tsui; ⏱ noon-3pm & 6pm-midnight; M Tsim Sha Tsui
This tarted-up erstwhile dive may look a swish and sleek but it still serves pretty authentic *rendang* (spicy beef), *gado-gado* (salad with peanut sauce) and other Indonesian favourites.

### ♙ KYOZASA 京笹居酒屋
*Japanese* $$

⏱ 2376 1888; 20 Ashley Rd, Tsim Sha Tsui; ⏱ noon-11pm Mon-Sat, noon-10pm Sun; M Tsim Sha Tsui
This colourful, cosy and relatively inexpensive Japanese restaurant has a menu that extends from sushi to steaks via hotpots. There are also reasonably priced set lunches.

### ♙ MERHABA 瑪哈巴
*Turkish* $$

☎ 2367 2263; ground fl, Yiu Pont House, 12 Knutsford Tce; ⏱ 4pm-2am Mon-Thu, 4pm-3am Fri & Sat, 4pm-midnight Sun; M Tsim Sha Tsui
This Turkish establishment with the exciting name of 'Hi' entertains with its Chinese belly dancer (Tuesday to Saturday). As always at Turkish restaurants, it would behove you to stick with the meze and the *raki* (anis-flavoured aperitif) and eschew the main courses.

### 🍴 SUSHI ONE 一壽司
*Japanese* $

☎ 2155 0633; 23 Ashley Rd, Tsim Sha Tsui; ⏱ noon-midnight; Ⓜ Tsim Sha Tsui

This new sushi place with a mesmerising fish-tank wall has become the hang-out of choice among the trendy *habitués* of Ashley Rd.

### 🍴 SWEET DYNASTY
糖朝甜品專門店 *Nov 6/08*
*Cantonese* $

☎ 2199 7799; 88 Canton Rd, Tsim Sha Tsui; ⏱ 10am-midnight Mon-Thu, 10am-1pm Fri, 7.30-1am Sat, 7.30am-midnight Sun; Ⓜ Tsim Sha Tsui

This simple Cantonese place has it all – from fine dim sum (served only on weekends) to tofu soups to bowls of congee big enough to swim in. It's a bun fight at lunch time but somehow, amidst all the noise and clatter and kids, the Sweet Dynasty retains a sense of style. *Mmm congee + Beer gung hor!*

### 🍴 WILDFIRE *Italian, Pizza* $

☎ 3690 1598; ground fl, Carlton Bldg, 2-3 Knutsford Tce, Tsim Sha Tsui; ⏱ noon-3pm daily, 6pm-1am Sun -Thu, 6pm-3am Fri & Sat; Ⓜ Tsim Sha Tsui

This Italian place is a safe and popular bet on Knutsford Tce, serving excellent pizzas and enough skewered meat to satisfy a ravenous army.

### 🍴 WU KONG SHANGHAI RESTAURANT 滬江飯店
*Shanghainese* $$

☎ 2366 7244; basement, Alpha House, 27-33 Nathan Rd, Tsim Sha Tsui; ⏱ 11.30am-midnight; Ⓜ Tsim Sha Tsui

The specialities at this Shanghainese restaurant – cold pigeon in wine sauce and crispy fried eels – are worth a trip across town. Dim sum is served all day.

### 🍴 XTC GELATO *Ice-cream Parlour* $

☎ 2368 3602; Star Ferry Terminal, Tsim Sha Tsui; ⏱ 11am-midnight; 🚢 Star Ferry (Tsim Sha Tsui)

OK, it's just ice cream (sorry, gelato) but it *is* good. Choose from up to 20 exotic flavours, including ginger with cinnamon, mango and guava.

## 🍸 DRINK

In general, Kowloon has more of a local Chinese scene than Hong Kong Island. There are four basic clusters of bars in Tsim Sha Tsui: along Ashley Rd; within the triangle formed by Hanoi Rd, Prat Ave and Chatham Rd; up along Knutsford Tce, Kowloon's tame answer to Lan Kwai Fong; and most recently along Minden Ave behind the Holiday Inn. Tsim Sha Tsui East is swanky hostess-bar territory for the most part.

bar you'll have already started marvelling at the view. Don't take flight: sit down in a scoop chair, sip a drink and scoff international snacks.

# ⭐ PLAY

## ⭐ HARI'S *Live Music & Bar*

☎ 2369 3111 ext 1345; mezzanine, Holiday Inn Golden Mile, 50 Nathan Rd, Tsim Sha Tsui; 🕐 5.30pm-2am, happy hour 5.30-9pm Mon-Sat, all evening Sun; Ⓜ Tsim Sha Tsui

Tacky, classy or neither? You decide after you've had a couple of speciality martinis (there are over a dozen to challenge you). There's live music nightly, from 6.15pm and again at 8.45pm Monday to Saturday and from 7.30pm on Sunday.

## ⭐ HONG KONG CULTURAL CENTRE 香港文化中心

*Concert hall & Theatre*

☎ 2734 2009; www.hkculturalcentre .gov.hk; 10 Salisbury Rd, Tsim Sha Tsui; tickets $100-500; Ⓜ Tsim Sha Tsui (exit E) 🚢 Star Ferry (Tsim Sha Tsui)

This odd building clad in pink ceramic tiles is one of Hong

Hong Kong Cultural Centre

Kong's most distinctive – if not loved – landmarks. Nonetheless the centre is a world-class venue – in fact, Hong Kong's premier venue – with a 2000-seat concert hall with impressive Rieger pipe organ, two theatres, rehearsal studios and an impressive main lobby. It's home to the Hong Kong Philharmonic and the Hong Kong Chinese Orchestra, and major touring companies play here. There are daily tours ($10/5); phone ahead.

### ⭐ MAMA'S *Club*
☎ 2368 2121; 4-5 Knutsford Tce, Tsim Sha Tsui; 🕐 4pm-3am Sun-Thu, 4pm-4am Fri & Sat, happy hour 4-9pm & midnight-3am Sun-Thu, 4-9pm Fri & Sat; Ⓜ Tsim Sha Tsui

Mama's theme is tropical-island-ish and, unusually for most late-night watering holes, it's a friendly spot. On Friday and Saturday nights there's a DJ and a young crowd shaking their thing out on the postage-stamp-sized dance floor.

### ⭐ NED KELLY'S LAST STAND
*Live Music & Bar*
☎ 2376 0562; 11A Ashley Rd, Tsim Sha Tsui; 🕐 11.15am-2am, happy hour 11.15am-9pm; Ⓜ Tsim Sha Tsui 🚢 Star Ferry (Tsim Sha Tsui)

Ashley Rd in Tsim Sha Tsui has its own little time warp in this tribute to the 19th-century Australian bushranger and folk hero. A great tradition continues with the Kelly Gang playing Dixieland jazz nightly from 9.30pm till 1am.

### ⭐ NEW WALLY MATT LOUNGE *(Gay) Club*
☎ 2721 2568; 5A Humphrey's Ave; 🕐 5pm-4am, happy hour 5-10pm; Ⓜ Tsim Sha Tsui

The name comes from the old Waltzing Matilda pub, one of the daggiest gay watering holes in creation and where a French friend swears that the escargots on his plate had been plucked from the walls of that dark and dank place. But New Wally Matt is an upbeat and busy place, with internet access and a pubby atmosphere.

# >KOWLOON: YAU MA TEI & MONG KOK

Just north of what locals called 'Tsimsy' is Yau Ma Tei (pronounced yow-ma-day and meaning 'Place of Sesame Plants'). The district's narrow byways are good places to check out Hong Kong's more traditional urban society and there are some interesting walks to take along the streets running east to west between Kansu St and Jordan Rd, including Nanking St (mahjong shops and parlours), Ning Po St (paper kites and votives, such as houses, mobile phones and hell money, to burn for the dead) and Saigon St (herbalist shops, old-style tailors, pawnshops). On Shanghai St you'll find Chinese bridal and trousseau shops. Mong Kok (Prosperous Point) is one of Hong Kong's most congested working-class residential areas, as well as one of its busiest shopping districts. It is rapidly getting a face-lift, spurred on by the opening of the Langham Place shopping mall.

## YAU MA TEI & MONG KOK

### ◉ SEE
Flower Market ..................... 1 C1
Jade Market ......................... 2 B5
Jade Market ......................... 3 B5
Shanghai St Artspace ........ 4 B4
Temple Street Night
Market ................................... 5 B4
Temple Street Night
Market ................................... 6 B5
Tin Hau Temple .................. 7 B5
Tung Choi St (Ladies')
Market ................................... 8 B3
Yuen Po St Bird
Garden .................................. 9 C1

### ▢ SHOP
Co-op ..................................... 10 B3
Mong Kok Computer
Centre ................................... 11 C3
Rag Brochure ................. (see 12)
Trendy Zone ..................... 12 B3
Winframe System ....... (see 11)
Wise Mount Sports ........ 13 C3
Yue Hwa Chinese
Products Emporium ........ 14 B6

### ⭐ PLAY
Broadway
Cinematheque ................. 22 B5

### 🍴 EAT
Good Hope Noodle ........ 15 D2
Kubrick Bookshop
Cafe ....................................... 16 B5
Mido ...................................... 17 B5
Ming Court .......................... 18 B3
Pak Bo Vegetarian
Kitchen ................................. 19 B1
Peking Restaurant .......... 20 C6
Saint's Alp Teahouse ..... 21 B3

# ◉ SEE

## ◉ JADE MARKET 玉器市場
**Kansu & Battery Sts, Yau Ma Tei;**
🕙 **10am-6pm;** Ⓜ **Yau Ma Tei (exit C),**
**Jordan (exit A)** 🚌 **9**
This market, split into two parts by the loop formed by Battery St, has hundreds of stalls selling all varieties and grades of jade. Unless you really know your nephrite from your jadeite, though, it's not wise to buy expensive pieces here.

## ◉ SHANGHAI ST ARTSPACE 上海街視藝空間
☎ **2770 2157; www.ssa06.org; 404**
**Shanghai St, Mong Kok; admission free;**
🕙 **11am-2pm & 3-8pm Tue-Sun;** Ⓜ **Yau**
**Ma Tei (exit A1), Mong Kok (exit E1)**
Funded by the Hong Kong Arts Development Council, this exhibition hall is a small venue in an unusual location and concentrates on cutting-edge new art by local artists. Video assemblages, photography, computer art and mixed media all get coverage.

## ◉ TEMPLE ST NIGHT MARKET 廟街夜市
**Temple St (btwn Jordan Rd & Man Ming**
**Lane), Yau Ma Tei;** 🕙 **4pm-midnight;**
Ⓜ **Jordan, Yau Ma Tei (exit C), Jordan**
**(exit C2)**
Temple St, which extends from Man Ming Lane in the north to Nanking St in the south and is cut in two by the Tin Hau temple complex, is the place to go for cheap clothes, *dai pai dong* (open-air street stall) food, watches, pirate CDs and DVDs, fake labels, footwear, cookware and everyday items. Any marked prices should be considered mere suggestions – this is definitely a place to bargain. It's also a place of entertainment (left).

## ◉ TIN HAU TEMPLE 天后廟
☎ **2332 9240; cnr Public Square St &**
**Nathan Rd, Yau Ma Tei; admission free;**
🕙 **8am-5pm;** Ⓜ **Yau Ma Tei (exit C)**
A couple of blocks northeast of the Jade Market (left) is this temple, which is dedicated to Tin Hau, the goddess of seafarers. You'll find a row of fortune-tellers, some of whom speak English, if you head through the last doorway on the right from the main entrance on Public Square St. An incense spiral that lasts a generous 10 days will set you back a mere $130.

---

### WHEN WE WERE MEN
The Temple St Night Market used to be known as 'Men's St' because the market only sold men's clothing. This was to distinguish it from the 'Ladies' Market' (or 'Women's St') on Tung Choi St to the northeast in Mong Kok.

---

Market stall, Yau Ma Tei

##  TUNG CHOI ST (LADIES') MARKET 通菜街（女人街）

**Tung Choi St (btwn Argyle & Dundas Sts), Mong Kok;** ⊙ **noon-10.30pm;** Ⓜ **Mong Kok (exit D3)**

Also known as Ladies' Market, the Tung Choi St market is a cheek-by-jowl affair offering up cheap clothes and trinkets. Vendors start setting up their stalls as early as noon, but it's best to get here between 1pm and 6pm when there's much more on offer.

## YUEN PO ST BIRD GARDEN & FLOWER MARKET 園圃街雀鳥花園及花墟

**Yuen Po St (btwn Boundary St & Flower Market Rd), Mong Kok;** ⊙ **7am-8pm;** Ⓜ **Prince Edward (exit B1)** Ⓡ **Mong Kok KCR East Rail** 🚌 **1, 1A, 2C, 12A**

There are hundreds of birds for sale at the Yuen Po St Bird Garden, along with elaborate birdcages carved from teak and bamboo. The Chinese have long

## DESIGNER THREADS À LA HONG KONG

Generally not well funded, Hong Kong's fashion designers exist like nomads, constantly on the move to where rents are low. This usually means dingy arcades with narrow corridors and shoebox units. Wherever they settle, loyalists flock in, rents go up, and they relocate again. This cycle is very much completed at Beverley Commercial Centre and Rise Commercial Centre in Tsim Sha Tsui – both had their heydays in the 1980s and '90s. New centres have since sprung up.

Although Soho is an established dining district, it's a new frontier for fashion. Shops here cater to a relatively affluent clientele that includes young urban professionals and tourists.

> **Co-op** (Map p129; ☎ 3580 1092; Shop 916, 9th fl, Langham Pl, 555 Shanghai St, Mong Kok; ⏰ 12.30-11pm; Ⓜ Mong Kok) Co-op in the Langham Place shopping mall, the upper floors of which boast a selection of compact boutiques with affordable items, features young fashion pieces, including T-shirts printed with local slang and motifs ($150), jeans ($450) and checked shirts.

> **Dialogue** (Map p57; ☎ 2540 3101; 49 Staunton St, Soho; ⏰ noon-9pm; Ⓜ Central) One of the very first boutiques in Soho, Dialogue offers stylish all-day menswear items. Dress shirts are $860, ties $380.

> **Spy Soho** (Map p57; ☎ 2317 6928; 21 Staunton St, Central; ⏰ noon-10pm; Ⓜ Central) This branch of Causeway Bay's Spy (p99) by Henry Lau, the local designer who pioneered the Rise Commercial Centre (where the original shop remains), features plusher items for both men and women. Funky print T-shirts are $400, evening wear $6900, signature embroidered jeans $998.

*Reggie Ho, South China Morning Post journalist*

favoured songbirds as pets, and a bird's singing prowess will often determine its price. Some species of birds are also considered harbingers of good fortune, which is why you'll sometimes see them being taken to the races. If you carry on walking south along Yuen Po St, you'll reach the daily flower market, where some 50 florists sell blooms and plants. To see the flower market at its busiest, head there after 10am, especially on Sundays.

## 🛍 SHOP

These districts – Mong Kok in particular – have a number of streets selling only one or two types of goods. Fife St, for example, has an amazing collection of stalls selling old vinyl, books, ceramics, machinery and music scores. The northern end of Tung Choi St, on the other hand, is awash in shops selling goldfish (important in feng shui!) and bicycles. The street markets in Yau

Ma Tei and Mong Kok have the cheapest clothes in town.

###  MONG KOK COMPUTER CENTRE
旺角電腦中心 *Computers*

**8-8A Nelson St, Mong Kok;** 🕙 **10am-11pm;** Ⓜ **Mong Kok**

Three floors of computer shops. Though geared more towards the Cantonese-speaking market than the foreign one, you can generally get better deals than in Tsim Sha Tsui. Check **Winframe System** ( ☎ 2300 1238; Shop 106-107, 1st fl).

### 🔲 TRENDY ZONE 潮流特區
*Clothing & Accessories*

**Chow Tai Fook Centre, 580A Nathan Rd, Mong Kok;** Ⓜ **Mong Kok**

This micromall is one of the most successful in Hong Kong and is full of tiny shops selling new and vintage gear for guys and gals. **Rag Brochure** ( ☎ 2391 4660; Shop 4, basement; 🕙 1.30-10pm) is one of the better shops in the mall.

### 🔲 WISE MOUNT SPORTS
惠峰運動用品公司 *Sporting Goods*

☎ **2787 3011; www.wisemount.com.hk; 75 Sai Yee St, Mong Kok;** 🕙 **noon-10pm;** Ⓜ **Mong Kok**

A reputable family-run shop with camping gear, swimming goggles, pocket knives, compasses, hard-wearing bags and sports trophies.

Kubrick Bookshop Cafe (p134)

### 🔲 YUE HWA CHINESE PRODUCTS EMPORIUM
裕華國貨 *Department Store*

☎ **3511 2222; www.yuehwa.com; 301-309 Nathan Rd, Yau Ma Tei;** 🕙 **10am-10pm;** Ⓜ **Jordan**

This cavernous place is everything a visiting souvenir-hunter could ask for – seven packed floors of ceramics, furniture, souvenirs and clothing, as well as bolts of silk, herbs, clothes, porcelain, luggage, umbrellas and kitchenware. It's the biggest and best of some 18 branches of Yue Hwa across Hong Kong.

# 🍴 EAT

## 🍴 GOOD HOPE NOODLE

好旺角粥麵家 *Noodle Bar*  $

☎ 2394 5967; 146 Sai Yeung Choi St South, Mong Kok; 🕙 11am-3am; Ⓜ Mong Kok

This busy noodle-stop is known far and wide for its terrific won ton soups and shredded pork noodles with spicy bean sauce. Good Hope Noodle is an eat-and-go sort of place so don't come here if you feel like lingering.

## 🍴 KUBRICK BOOKSHOP CAFE *Café*  $

☎ 2384 5465; Shop H2, Prosperous Garden, 3 Public Square St, Yau Ma Tei; 🕙 11.30am-10pm; Ⓜ Yau Ma Tei

This café and bookshop next to the Broadway Cinematheque (opposite) has a great range of film-related books, magazines and paraphernalia, and serves good coffee and decent pre-flick food such as sandwiches ($33 to $42) and pasta ($35 to $45).

## 🍴 MIDO 美都餐室

*Hong Kong Fast Food*  $

☎ 2384 6402; 63 Temple St, Yau Ma Tei; 🕙 7.30am-10pm; Ⓜ Yau Ma Tei

This ultimate version of a *cha chan tang,* a uniquely Hong Kong café with local dishes, in a 1950s building opposite the Tin Hau Temple (p130) serves meals throughout the day, but it's best to come at

Broadway Cinematheque sign

breakfast ($15 to $30) or in the afternoon for such oddities as *yuan yang* (equal parts coffee and black tea with milk), *ling lok* (boiled cola with lemon and ginger) and toast smeared with condensed milk.

### 🍴 MING COURT 明閣
*Cantonese*                                    $$$$
☎ 3552 3388; 6th fl, Langham Place Hotel, 555 Shanghai St, Mong Kok; ⏰ 11am-3pm & 6-10.30pm; Ⓜ Mong Kok
This restaurant in the flash Langham Place Hotel serves excellent modern Cantonese fare in a lovely dining room surrounded by replicas of ancient pottery unearthed in the area. Dim sum is served at lunch daily.

### 🍴 PAK BO VEGETARIAN KITCHEN 百寶齋廚
*Vegetarian Chinese*                            $
☎ 2380 2681; ground fl, Lee Tat Bld, 785-785A Nathan Rd, Mong Kok; ⏰ 11am-11pm; Ⓜ Mong Kok
This simple vegetarian restaurant up near Boundary St isn't really worth a detour, but it is here should you be dragging the streets and eschewing meats in Mong Kok.

### 🍴 PEKING RESTAURANT 北京酒樓
*Northern Chinese*                              $$
☎ 2730 1315; 1st fl, 227 Nathan Rd, Yau Ma Tei; ⏰ 11.30am-11pm; Ⓜ Jordan

This no-frills restaurant keeps Peking duck fans merrily chomping away. If the Peking duck ($320) doesn't do it for you, try the Northern-style crab dishes and pastries.

### 🍴 SAINT'S ALP TEAHOUSE 仙跡岩 *Chinese Snacks*     $
☎ 2782 1438; 61A Shantung St, Mong Kok; ⏰ 11.30am-12.30am Sun-Thu, 11.30am-1am Fri & Sat; Ⓜ Mong Kok
One in a chain of clean and very cheap snackeries in Hong Kong (look for the footprint logo). It's a great pit stop for Taiwanese-style frothy tea with tapioca drops and Chinese snacks such as shrimp balls, noodles and rice puddings.

## ⭐ PLAY

### ☆ BROADWAY CINEMATHEQUE 百老匯電影中心 *Cinema*
☎ 2388 3188; www.cinema.com.hk; ground fl, Prosperous Garden, 3 Public Square St, Yau Ma Tei; tickets $32-55; Ⓜ Yau Ma Tei
Yau Ma Tei may seem like an unlikely place for an alternative cinema, but it's worth checking out for new art-house releases and re-runs here. The Kubrick Bookshop Cafe (opposite) next door serves good coffee and food.

# 👁 SEE

## 👁 CHI LIN NUNNERY
志蓮淨苑

☎ 2354 1604; 5 Chi Lin Dr, Diamond Hill; admission free; 🕐 nunnery 9am-5pm, garden 6.30am-7pm; Ⓜ Diamond Hill (exit C2, then a 5min walk along Fung Tak Rd)

This Tang-style wooden complex, built in 1998, is a serene place with lotus ponds, bonsai and silent nuns delivering offerings to Buddha and arhats (Buddhist disciples freed from the cycle of birth and death). Designed to show the harmony of humans with nature, the complex is pretty convincing until you spy the high-rises looming above.

## 👁 KOWLOON WALLED CITY PARK 九龍寨城公園

☎ 2716 9962; www.lcsd.gov.hk /parks/kwcp/en/index.php; Tung Tsing Rd, Kowloon City; admission free; 🕐 6.30am-11pm; Ⓜ Lok Fu (exit B, then 15min walk south on Junction & Tung Tau Tsuen Rds) 🚌 1, 10, 113

The walls that enclose this beautiful park were once the perimeter of a notorious village that technically remained part of China throughout British rule. The enclave was known for its vice,

Chi Lin Nunnery

## HONG KONG'S OWN BLOSSOM

The flower on Hong Kong's flag is the *Bauhinia blakeana*, also called the Hong Kong orchid. This species of bauhinia exists nowhere else. From early November to March you may see the purple blossoms on bauhinia trees, a species unique to the territory, in Victoria Park (p97), Kowloon Walled City Park (p138) or outside the Foreign Correspondents' Club (Map p57, D5) in Central.

prostitution, gambling and – worst of all – illegal dentists. In 1984 the Hong Kong government acquired the area, rehoused the residents elsewhere and replaced the tenements with pavilions, ponds, turtles, goldfish and exquisite flora. The park opened in 1996.

### ⚫ LEI CHENG UK HAN TOMB MUSEUM

李鄭屋漢墓博物館

☎ 2386 2863; http://hk.history .museum; 41 Tonkin St, Sham Shui Po; admission free; ⏰ 10am-6pm Mon-Wed, Fri & Sat, 1-6pm Sun; Ⓜ Cheung Sha Wan (exit A3, then 10min northeast along Tonkin St) 🚌 2

This burial vault, dating from the Eastern Han dynasty (AD 25–220) and central to the museum, was discovered in 1955 when workers were levelling the hillside for a housing estate. The tomb is

encased in a concrete shell for protection and you can only peek through a plastic window. The museum also contains some 58 pottery and bronze pieces taken from the tomb.

### ⚫ SIK SIK YUEN WONG TAI SIN TEMPLE

嗇色園黃大仙祠

☎ 2854 4333; Lung Cheung Rd, Wong Tai Sin; donation requested; ⏰ 7am-6pm; Ⓜ Wong Tai Sin (exit B2)

This large and very active Taoist temple was built in 1973 and dedicated to the god Wong Tai Sin, who is worshipped by business-people, the sick, and those trying to avoid illness. It's one of the busiest temples in Hong Kong and a great place to visit to get an idea of how Hong Kong people worship.

## STICKY FORTUNES

There are any number of props and implements that Chinese use to predict the future, but the most popular method of divination in Hong Kong is the *chim* (fortune sticks), found at Buddhist and Taoist temples, including Sik Sik Yuen Wong Tai Sin Temple. The sticks are shaken out of a box on to the ground; each bears a numeral corresponding to a printed slip of paper in a set held by the temple guardian. That slip of paper should be taken to the temple's fortune-teller, who can interpret its particular meaning for you.

Moon Gate at Kowloon Walled City Park (p138)

# 🛍 SHOP

## 💻 GOLDEN COMPUTER ARCADE 黃金電腦商場
*Computers*

**Basement & 1st fl, 146-152 Fuk Wa St, Sham Shui Po;** Ⓜ **Sham Shui Po**
Shops in the centre sell computers and components as well as cheap software and accessories such as keyboards, ink cartridges, CDs and DVDs. Most shops open daily from 10am to 10pm but some don't open until noon. It's packed at the weekend.

# 🍴 EAT

## 🍴 KOWLOON CITY THAI RESTAURANTS
友誼泰國菜館 *Thai*        $-$$

🚌 **5C, 101**
The neighbourhood of Kowloon City is Hong Kong's Thai quarter, and it's worth a journey if you're looking for a *tom yum* or green-curry fix. Among the simplest and most authentic of the restaurants here is **Friendship Thai Food** ( ☎ 2382 8671; 38 Kai Tak Rd; ⏰ 3pm-midnight), which attracts Thai maids by the mop-and-bucketful. Nearby, the **Golden Orchard Thai Restaurant** ( ☎ 2383 3076; 12 Lung Kong Rd; ⏰ noon-midnight) has spill-over rooms for when its restaurant fills up. **Wong Chun Chun Thai Restaurant** ( ☎ 2716 6269; ground & 1st fl, Belshine Centre, 23 Tak Ku Ling Rd; ⏰ 11am-2am) is one of the largest restaurants in Kowloon City and keeps later hours than most of its competition.

The surrounding neighbourhood is packed with herbalists, jewellers, tea merchants and bird shops; it's worth having a post-prandial meander to take a look.

# >NEW TERRITORIES

The New Territories, so called because it was leased to Britain in 1898, (almost half a century after Hong Kong Island and four decades after Kowloon were ceded to the crown) is large, comprising 747 sq km, or almost 68% of Hong Kong's land area. For many years the area was Hong Kong's rural hinterland, but since WWII, at which time some 80% of the land was under cultivation, many parts of the NT – as it's known locally – have become increasingly urbanised. In the past two decades the speed at which this development has taken place has been nothing short of heart stopping. In the past, the biggest impediment to growth in the New Territories was a lack of good transport. Nowadays, with the advent of the second branch of the KCR (Kowloon–Canton Railway), getting to the New Territories has never been easier. Country parks, a world-class museum, one of Hong Kong's most interesting monasteries and a new wetland centre are among the attractions here.

# NEW TERRITORIES

## 👁 SEE

Hong Kong Heritage
Museum .........................**1** C3
Hong Kong Wetland
Park ...............................**2** B5
MacLehose Trail ...........**3** C3

Pak Tam Chung.............**4** C2
Sai Kung .......................**5** C2
Ten Thousand Buddhas
Monastery ....................**6** C3
Yuen Long ....................**7** B5

## 🍽 EAT

Jaspa's .........................(See 5)
Tung Kee Seafood
Restaurant ..................(See 5)
Koh-I-Noor ...................**8** C3

NEIGHBOURHOODS

NEW TERRITORIES

# SEE

## HONG KONG HERITAGE MUSEUM 香港文化博物館

☎ 2180 8188; www.heritagemuseum.gov.hk; 1 Man Lam Rd, Sha Tin; adult/child $10/5, free Wed; ☼ 10am-6pm Mon & Wed-Sat, 10am-7pm Sun; ⓡ Sha Tin KCR East Rail, then 10min walk west & south along Tai Po Rd & Lion Rock Tunnel Rd

Housed in a three-storey purpose-built structure, this award-winning museum has magnificent displays on Cantonese opera and the cultural heritage of the New Territories, the Children's Discovery Gallery (which has learning and play zones) and a gallery for the impressive art collection of one Dr TT Tsui. There are five thematic (ie temporary) galleries as well.

## HONG KONG WETLAND PARK 香港濕地公園

☎ 3152 2666, 2708 8885; www.wetlandpark.com; Wetland Park Rd, Tin Shui Wai; adult/child $30/15; ☼ 10am-5pm Wed-Mon; ⓡ KCR West Rail to Tin Shui Wai then Light Rail 705 or 706, 🚌 967

This 61-hectare ecological park in Tin Shui Wai north of Tuen Mun, focuses on the wetland ecosystems and biodiversity of the northwest New Territories, and is a wonderful place to spend an entertaining (and educational) morning or afternoon (above). To

A golden Buddha at Ten Thousand Buddhas Monastery

reach the park, take the KCR West Rail to Tin Shui Wai and board Light Rail line 705 or 706. Bus 967 from the Admiralty MTR (Mass Transit Rail) bus station on Hong Kong Island also serves the park.

## SAI KUNG 西貢

Ⓜ Choi Hung then minibus 1A or 1M, 🚌 92, ⓡ Sha Tin KCR East Rail then 299

Apart from the Outlying Islands, the Sai Kung Peninsula is one of the last havens left in Hong Kong for hikers, swimmers and boaters, and most of it is one huge 7500-hectare country park. A short journey to any of the islands off Sai Kung town is rewarding. Hidden away are some excellent beaches that can be visited by *kaido* (small boats), which depart from the waterfront. The MacLehose Trail, a 100km route across the New Territories, begins at Pak Tam Chung on the Sai Kung Peninsula. On top of this Sai Kung town boasts excellent bars and restaurants, especially along the attractive waterfront.

### ☉ TEN THOUSAND BUDDHAS MONASTERY 萬佛寺

☎ 2691 1067; Sha Tin; admission free; ⏰ 9am-5pm; ☒ Sha Tin KCR East Rail
Built in the 1950s, this large complex actually contains more than 10,000 Buddhas – some 12,800 miniature statues line the walls of the main temple, in fact. Dozens of life-sized golden statues of Buddha's followers flank the steep steps leading to the monastery complex. There is also a nine-storey pagoda. The monastery sits atop Po Fook Hill about 500m northwest of Sha Tin KCR East Rail

---

#### MIDAS TOUCH

The mummy under glass in the main temple of the Ten Thousand Buddhas Monastery is the embalmed body of Yuet Kai (1878–1965), the monastery's founder. He was so revered that upon his death his corpse was encased in gold leaf. The box next to the bier collects donations for the temple's – and the Venerable Yuet's – upkeep.

---

station. Take exit B and walk down the ramp. Turn left onto Pai Tau St and then right onto Sheung Wo Che St. At the end of this road, a series of signs in English will direct you to the left along a concrete path to the first of some 400 steps up to the complex.

## 🍴 EAT

### 🍴 JASPA'S

*International & Fusion* $$
☎ 2792 6388; 13 Sha Tsui Path, Sai Kung; ⏰ 8.30am-midnight; 🚌 92, 299
Jaspa's is an upbeat, casual place serving international and fusion food to a motley crowd.

### 🍴 KOH-I-NOOR *Indian* $$
☎ 2601 4969; Shop A181-182, 1st fl, New Town Plaza Phase III, Sha Tin; ⏰ noon-3pm & 6-11.30pm ☒ Sha Tin KCR
This popular place is a good and stylish choice for Northern Indian food.

### 🍴 TUNG KEE SEAFOOD RESTAURANT 通記海鮮野味酒家
*Chinese & Seafood* $$$
☎ 2792 7453; 96-102 Man Nin St, Sai Kung; ⏰ 9am-midnight; 🚌 92, 299
This is the pick of the crop for Cantonese seafood in Sai Kung. It's not cheap, of course, but the food is outstanding. Make sure to call ahead.

# >OUTLYING ISLANDS

Hong Kong's islands vary greatly in size, appearance and character. While many are little more than uninhabited rocks poking out of the South China Sea, Lantau is almost twice the size of Hong Kong Island. Because they are so sparsely populated, the Outlying Islands are the territory's escape routes and its playgrounds. From the tranquil lanes of Cheung Chau to the monasteries and country parks of Lantau, and the waterfront seafood restaurants of Lamma, Hong Kong's islands offer a world of peace and quiet along with a host of sights and activities. What's more, some of Hong Kong's best beaches punctuate the rocky coasts.

The islands listed here are all easily accessible from Hong Kong Island daily, and Cheung Chau and Lantau can be reached from Kowloon at the weekend as well.

## OUTLYING ISLANDS

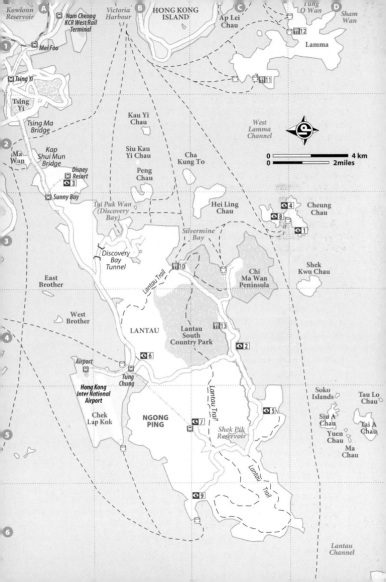

# SEE

## CHEUNG CHAU 長洲

🚢 Cheung Chau from Central (pier 5, Outlying Islands ferry terminal) or Tsim Sha Tsui (Star Ferry pier, weekends only)

The houseboats bobbing up and down Cheung's Chau's busy harbour are one attraction here but make sure you also see **Pak Tai Temple** ( ☎ 2981 0663; Pak She Fourth Lane; ☉ 9am-5pm), site of the colourful Bun Festival (below) in May, swim at **Kwun Yam Wan (Afternoon) Beach** (which is also popular with windsurfers) and visit **Cheung Po Tsai Cave** in the southwest corner, which was an old pirate hide-out.

## LAMMA ISLAND 南丫島

🚢 Yung Shue Wan or Sok Kwu Wan from Central (pier 4, Outlying Islands ferry terminal) or Aberdeen

The third-largest island after Lantau and Hong Kong, Lamma is known for its lively pubs, seafood restaurants, beaches and hikes.

The laid-back lifestyle, strong feeling of community and relatively low rental make it a popular place with expats. The most interesting way to see a good portion of the island is to follow the 4km-long Family Trail between the two main villages, Yung Shue Wan and Sok Kwu Wan, which takes a little over an hour, and return to Central by ferry from there.

Nov 2/08

## LANTAU ISLAND 大嶼山

🚢 Mui Wo from Central (pier 6, Outlying Islands ferry terminal) or Tsim Sha Tsui (Star Ferry pier at weekend only)

More than half of Lantau's surface area is designated country parkland, and there are several superb mountain trails, including the 70km **Lantau Trail**, which passes over both Lantau Peak (957m). There are also some excellent beaches including **Cheung Sha**, the longest in Hong Kong, some interesting traditional villages, such as **Tai O** on the west coast (which is famous

## GOING FOR THE BUNS

The eight-day Cheung Chau Bun Festival in May is renowned for the bun towers built near Pak Tai Temple (above). These are formed from bamboo scaffolding up to 20m high and covered with sacred rolls. Formerly, people would scramble up the towers on the designated day to grab one of the buns for good luck, but the practice stopped after a fatal accident in 1978. In 2005 the tower-climbing event was revived as a race with extra safety precautions. On the third day of the festival (a Sunday), there's a lively procession of floats, stilt walkers and colourfully dressed 'floating children' who are carried through the streets on long poles that are cleverly wired to metal supports hidden under their clothing.

Tian Tan Buddha statue

for its rope-tow ferry and pungent shrimp paste) and several important religious retreats, including the **Po Lin Monastery** (admission free; ☿ 6am-6pm) and the adjacent **Tian Tan Buddha** (admission free; ☿ 10am-5.30pm), the largest outdoor Buddha statue in the world. Adjacent to the complex is **Ngong Ping Village** ( ☎ 2109 9179; www.np360.com.hk; admission free; ☿ 10am-6pm Mon-Fri, 10am-6.30pm Sat & Sun), with several Buddhist-related multimedia attractions, including Walking with Buddha and Monkey's Tale Theatre (adult/child $65/35 for both), shops and food outlets, and served by the **Ngong Ping Skyrail** (adult/child $58/28 $88/45, one-way return) cable car from Tung Chung. Lantau's newest attraction is **Hong Kong Disneyland** ( ☎ 830 830; www.hongkongdisneyland.com; adult/child Mon-Fri $295/210, Sat & Sun $350/250;

☿ 10am-9pm Apr-Oct, 10am-7pm Nov-Mar), located on the northeast coast and served by its own MTR (Mass Transit Rail) station. For more information see left.

## GREEN TURTLES & EGGS

Sham Wan on Lamma's southern coast has traditionally been the one beach in the whole of Hong Kong where endangered green turtles (*Chelonia mydas*) still struggle onto the sand to lay their eggs from early June to the end of August. Along with developers, a major hurdle faced by the long-suffering turtles is the appetite of Lamma locals for their eggs. In 1994, three turtles laid about 200 eggs, which were promptly consumed by villagers. Nowadays anyone taking, possessing or attempting to sell one of the eggs faces a fine of $100,000 and one year in prison.

# >MACAU

Only an hour's boat ride to the west of Hong Kong, this charming fusion of Asian and Mediterranean cultures makes a magnificent getaway. The first European enclave in Asia, Macau was returned to Chinese sovereignty in 1999 after four-and-a-half centuries of Portuguese rule. The tiny (27.5 sq km) territory consists of the Macau Peninsula, which is attached to China, and the islands, Taipa and Coloane, connected by bridges to the mainland and to each other by an ever growing reclaimed land area called Cotai. About 95% of the population is ethnic Chinese and most visitors are gamblers drawn to the casinos. But Macau boasts picture-postcard churches and civil buildings, narrow streets, traditional shops and Portuguese and Macanese restaurants. And getting to Macau from Hong Kong has never been easier, with high-speed ferries now running between the two territories every half-hour around the clock.

# MACAU

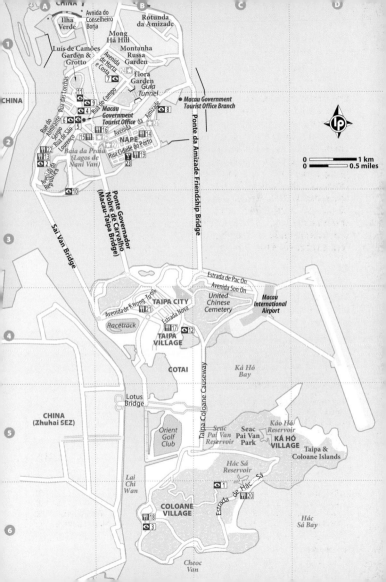

MACAU

# MACAU PENINSULA

## 👁 SEE

### 👁 A-MA TEMPLE 媽閣廟

**Templo de A-Ma; Rua de São Tiago da Barra; admission free; 🕙 10am-6pm**
North of Barra Hill, this 17th-century temple is dedicated to the goddess A-Ma, who is better known in Hong Kong as Tin Hau. At the main entrance is a large boulder with a coloured relief of a *lorcha* (a traditional sailing vessel).

### 👁 CHURCH OF ST DOMINIC 玫瑰堂

**Igreja de São Domingos; Largo de São Domingos; admission free; 🕙 8am-6pm**

Arguably the most beautiful in Macau, this 17th-century baroque church contains the **Treasury of Sacred Art** (Tresouro de Arte Sacra; ☎ 367 706; admission free; 🕙 10am-6pm), an Aladdin's cave of ecclesiastical art.

Lou Lim Ioc Garden

## ● LARGO DO SENADO
議事亭前地

**Avenida de Almeida Ribeiro**
'Senate Square', with its wavy
black-and-white cobbles and
beautiful colonial buildings, is the
heart and soul of Macau, and is
illuminated at night. Lovely **Holy
House of Mercy** (Santa Casa da Misericordia;
☎ 573 938; Travessa da Misericordia 2;
admission $5; 🕙 10am-1pm & 2.30-5.30pm
Mon-Sat), on the southeastern side
of the square, was a home for
orphans and prostitutes in the 18th
century. It's opposite Leal Senado.

## ● LEAL SENADO
民政總署大樓

**163 Avenida de Almeida Ribeiro; admis-
sion free; 🕙 gallery 9am-9pm Tue-Sun,
library 1-7pm Mon-Sat**
Macau's most important historical
building, the 'Loyal Senate' now
houses the mayor's office, an art
gallery and the ornately furnished
Senate Library. Above the entrance to the blue-tiled courtyard
garden is a heraldic inscription

---

**THIS WAY AROUND**

For info on getting to and from Macau
from Hong Kong see p191. Central
Macau is best explored on foot; taxis are
cheap for attractions further afield. The
*Macau Tourist Map*, available from any
Macau Government Tourist Information
branch, has a full list of bus routes.

---

dating from 1654 that refers to
Macau's support during Spain's
60-year occupation of Portugal.

## ● LOU LIM IOC GARDEN
盧廉若公園

**Jardim de Lou Lim Ioc; 10 Estrada de
Adolfo de Loureiro; admission free;
🕙 6am-9pm**
This wonderful garden has huge
shade trees, lotus ponds, bamboo
groves, grottoes and a bridge with
nine turns to escape from evil spirits
(who apparently can only move in
straight lines). Local people use the
park to practise t'ai chi or play traditional Chinese musical instruments.

## ● MACAU FISHERMAN'S
WHARF 澳門漁人碼頭

**Doca dos Pescadores de Macau; ☎ 299
3300; www.fishermanswharf.com.mo;
cnr Avenida de Amizade & Avenida Doutor
Sun Yat Sen; admission free; 🕙 24hr**
Built on 112 hectares of reclaimed
land in the Outer Harbour, this
kitsch 'theme park' is open all
hours and combines attractions,
hotels, shops and restaurants.

## ● MACAU MUSEUM
澳門博物館

**Museu de Macau; ☎ 357 911; Praceta do
Museu de Macau, Fortaleza do Monte;
adult/child $15/8, free on 15th of month;
🕙 10am-6pm Tue-Sun**
Housed in 17th-century Monte
Fort, this wonderful museum tells

MACAU

the story of the hybrid territory of Macau, with a host of multimedia exhibits focusing on its history, traditions and culture.

## MACAU TOWER
澳門旅遊塔

**Torre de Macau; ☎ 988 8656; www .macautower.com.mo; Largo da Torre de Macau; observation decks adult/child $70/35, climbs & walks from $30; ⏰ 10am -9pm Mon-Fri, 9am-9pm Sat & Sun**
At 338m, this is the 10th-tallest free-standing tower in the world.

The views across Macau's islands and city centre from the observation decks are spectacular, and the myriad climbs and walks on offer here cause much horror and hilarity.

## RUINS OF THE CHURCH OF ST PAUL 大三巴牌坊

**Ruinas de Igreja de São Paulo; Rua de São Paulo; admission free**
The façade and majestic stairway are all that remain of this church, which was designed by an Italian

Ruins of the Church of St Paul

Jesuit and built by exiled Japanese Christians in the early 17th century. However, with its wonderful statues, portals and engravings, some consider it to be the greatest monument to Christianity in Asia.

# 🍴 EAT

## 🍴 A LORCHA 船屋餐廳
*Portuguese* $$

☎ 313 193; 289A Rua do Almirante Sérgio; 🕑 12.30-3pm & 6.30-11pm Wed-Mon
The much loved 'Sailboat' restaurant facing the Inner Harbour northwest of Macau Tower has some of the best Portuguese food in Macau.

## 🍴 BOI NA BRASA *Brazilian* $

☎ 753 021; 1st fl, Nam Ngom Bldg, 188 Rua de Paris; 🕑 noon-3pm & 7.30-10.30pm Tue-Sun
Forget the menu at this cheerful, upbeat *churrascaria brasileira*

(Brazilian grill); just sit down and let the chef carve all manner of meat onto your plate. There are some buffet-style salads, but it's mainly a meat-fest.

## 🍴 CARAVELA 金船 *Pastries*

☎ 712 080; ground fl, Kam Loi Bldg, 7 Pátio do Comandante Mata e Oliveira; 🕑 8am-10pm Mon-Sat
This excellent *pastelaria* (pastry shop) – and hang-out of choice for Portuguese residents – just north of Avenida de Dom João IV is a bit tricky to find, but the delectable pastries and snacks make it worth the search.

## 🍴 CLUBE MILITAR DE MACAU 澳門陸軍俱樂部
*Portuguese* $$$

☎ 714 000; 975 Avenida da Praia Grande; 🕑 noon-3pm, 7-11pm
The Portuguese meals and other dishes served here may not be

---

## SHOPPING

While exploring the back lanes and streets of Macau Peninsula (B2), you'll stumble across bustling markets and traditional Chinese shops. Rua de Madeira is a charming market street, with many shops selling carved Buddha heads and other religious items. Rua dos Mercadores, which leads up to Rua da Tercena, will lead you past tailors, wok sellers, tiny jewellery shops, incense and mahjong shops, and other traditional businesses. At the far end of Rua da Tercena, where the road splits, is a flea market where you can pick up baskets and other rattan ware, jade pieces and old coins. Great streets for antiques, ceramics and curios (such as traditional Chinese kites) are Rua de São Paulo, Rua das Estalagens and Rua de São António, and the lanes off them. Most shops are open from 10.30am or 11am to 6pm or 7pm, with a one-hour lunchbreak some time between 12.30pm and 2pm.

the best in town, but the Macau Military Club is housed in one of the territory's most distinguished colonial buildings.

### 🍴 FAT SIU LAU 佛笑樓
*Macanese* $$

☎ 722 922; ground fl, Vista Magnífica Court Bldg, 1435 Avenida Doutor Sun Yat Sen; ☽ noon-3pm & 6.30pm-midnight
This very swish new branch of the long-established (since 1903!) 'House of the Smiling Buddha' on the waterfront of the reclaimed land area puts a modern spin on traditional local dishes such as codfish balls, African chicken and roast pigeon, and comes up trumps.

### 🍴 RESTAURANTE LITORAL
海灣餐廳 *Macanese* $$

☎ 967 878; 261A Rua do Almirante Sérgio; ☽ noon-3pm & 5.30-10.30pm
This is arguably the best Macanese restaurant on the peninsula, with superb duck and baked rice dishes.

## 🍸 DRINK

### 🍸 MOONWALKER BAR
夜光杯 *Bar*

☎ 751 326; ground fl, Vista Magnífica Court Bldg, 1435 Avenida Doutor Sun Yat Sen; ☽ 4pm-4am, happy hour 4-8pm
One of several watering holes on the waterfront, this place has live

entertainment most nights (usually Filipina chanteuses).

## ⭐ PLAY

### ⭐ BASEMENT *Club*

☎ 565 655; basement, 69 Av de Sidónio Pais; ☽ 9.30pm-4am Tue-Sat
The coolest lounge bar in town and playing some of the best tunes, this place has a great vibe, particularly at the weekend. It's a bit hard to find but just a short distance north-east of Lou Lim Ioc Garden. It's downstairs through a small arcade to the right of the BCM Bank.

### ⭐ CASINOS 娛樂場

Casinos, which now number two dozen with many more on the way, are the lifeblood of Macau. All operate 24 hours a day and punters must be over 18 and properly dressed. Standards are rising as competition increases, and even if you don't fancy playing the tables (in many the minimum bet is $100 or more), it's worth taking a look around, enjoying the free shows and just watching the way these temples to Mammon operate.
**Casino Lisboa** ( ☎ 375 111; Lisboa Hotel 2-4 Avenida de Lisboa), with its garish 1960s exterior, 'Chinese baroque' interior and decades of experience catering to Asia's high and low rollers, is the best known casino in Asia. It's quirky and charismatic in contrast with the vast new casinos. These

include the mammoth **Sands Macao Casino** ( ☎ 883 388; 203 Largo de Monte Carlo), with hundreds of slot and poker machines, more than 300 gaming tables, free drinks to gamblers and constant live entertainment. Vegas-style **Wynn Macau Casino** ( ☎ 889 966; Rua Cidade de Sintra) is the newest and flashiest of the lot, with every game imaginable (up to $2500 minimum bet) and original Matisse and Renoir paintings on the premises.

# TAIPA & COLOANE ISLANDS
## 👁 SEE

### 🟢 A-MA CULTURAL VILLAGE
媽祖文化村
**Vila Cultural de A-Ma, Alto de Coloane, Coloane;** ⏱ **8am-6pm**
A colossal 20m white-jade statue of the goddess who gave Macau its name sits atop Alto de Coloane (176m). Together with the enormous **Tian Hou Temple** ( ⏱ 8am-7.30pm) below, it forms the core of A-Ma Cultural Village, a cultural and religious complex containing a museum, a retreat and medical centres, a vegetarian restaurant and handicraft shops. A free bus departs for the village from the ornamental gate at the corner of Estrada Seac Pai Van and Estrada do Alto de Coloane every

Cars reflecting lights of Casino Lisboa

half-hour from 8am to 6pm.

### 🟢 CHAPEL OF ST FRANCIS XAVIER 聖方濟各教堂
**Capela de São Francisco Xavier Avenida de Cinco de Outubro, Coloane;** ⏱ **10am-8pm**
This delightful little church on the waterfront was built in 1928 to honour St Francis Xavier. He had been a missionary in Japan, and Japanese Catholics still come to Coloane to pay their respects.

### 🟢 TAIPA HOUSE MUSEUM
龍環葡韻住宅式博物館
**Casa Museum da Taipa;** ☎ **827 103 Avenida da Praia, Taipa; adult/child $5/3, free Sun;** ⏱ **10am-6pm Tue-Sun**

Espaçao Lisboa restaurant

The five lime green villas facing the water were built in 1921 by wealthy Macanese as summer residences and three of them collectively form this unusual museum, which has displays of costumes, and examines traditional ways of life in Portugal, the islands' traditional industries (fishing and the manufacture of oyster sauce, shrimp paste and fireworks) and Macanese domestic life in the early 20th century.

# 🍴 EAT

## 🍴 COZINHA PINÓCCHIO
木偶葡國餐廳 *Macanese* $$
☎ 827 128; 4 Rua do Sol, Taipa; ⏰ 11.45am-11.45pm
The place that launched the Taipa Village restaurant phenomenon, 'Pinocchio Kitchen' specialises in grilled fresh sardines, quail, pigeon and roast lamb.

## 🍴 ESPAÇAO LISBOA
里斯本地帶餐廳
*Portuguese* $$$
☎ 882 226, 6864200; 8 Rua dos Gaivotas, Coloane; ⏰ noon-3pm & 6.30-10pm Tue-Fri, noon-10.30pm Sat & Sun
The 'Lisbon Space' restaurant in a renovated village house

serves some of the most carefully prepared Portuguese dishes in Macau. Try the fish (swordfish, grouper etc) stewed in a *cataplana* (traditional copper pot), or the curried crab.

## 🍴 FERNANDO *Portuguese* $$
☎ 882 531; 9 Praia de Hác Sá; ⏰ noon-9.30pm
Famed for its seafood and idyllic waterfront location, Fernando has a devoted clientele and a pleasantly relaxed atmosphere – though it can get pretty crowded in the evening.

## 🍴 O CAPITULO 花窗餐廳
*Portuguese* $$
☎ 821 519; ground fl, Nam San Bldg, 154-156 Avenida de Kwong Tung, Taipa; ⏰ noon-10pm
This excellent eatery north of Macau Stadium serves absolutely scrumptious homemade Portuguese dishes that are made with the freshest of ingredients. At the weekend, try the roast suckling pig and the *fatias de Tomar*, a rich dessert made with egg yolks and syrup. For another sweet option, there's the *serradura* (saw dust) pudding – crumbled biscuits on a vanilla base.

Cliché it may be, but Hong Kong is a city that both works and plays hard, and the latter involves fine dining, drinking (to excess, some might say), shopping and communing with nature. This chapter will help you locate the best of these and many other pursuits by special category. It's subjective, yes. But we think you'll like it.

Hong Kong harbour

# ACCOMMODATION

There are three basic types of accommodation in Hong Kong: deluxe and top-end hotels, some of which count among the finest in the world; adequate but generally uninspiring midrange hotels; and cramped hostels and guesthouses at the budget level. Within each category there is a good deal of choice, and you should be able to find a comfortable place to stay at your price.

Hong Kong's deluxe hotels are special places, with individual qualities that propel them above the rest. Expect discreet, smooth-as-silk service, large bathtubs, superlative climate control, extensive cable TV and wireless internet access. They are most commonly found in Central and Admiralty on Hong Kong Island – though the Peninsula is in Tsim Sha Tsui.

Top-end hotels are in spiffy locations: they also have smart, comfortable rooms with excellent air-con, in-house movies and a good variety of room service options. Amenities include business facilities, bars and restaurants and fluent English-speaking staff. Tsim Sha Tsui East is chock-a-block with top-end places.

Midrange hotels tend to be generic business–tourist establishments with little to distinguish one from another. Rooms are spacious enough and usually have a bath, limited cable TV and room service. These are scattered around the territory, though you might try Wan Chai, Causeway Bay and Tsim Sha Tsui.

The majority of Hong Kong's budget digs are in Kowloon, with many on or near Nathan Rd. Though most budget rooms are very small, the places listed here are clean and cheerily shabby rather than grim and grimy.

haystack.lonelyplanet.com

Need a place to stay? Find and book it at lonelyplanet .com. More than 45 properties are featured for Hong Kong - each personally visited, thoroughly reviewed and happily recommended by a Lonely Planet author. From hostels to high-end hotels, we've hunted out the places that will bring you unique and special experiences. Read independent reviews by authors and other travellers, and get practical information including amenities, maps and photos. Then reserve your room simply and securely via Haystack - our online booking service. It's all at www.lonelyplanet.com/accommodation.

Hong Kong's two accommodation high seasons are from March to April and October to November, though things can be tight around Chinese New Year (late January or February) as well. Outside these periods, rates drop (sometimes substantially) and little extras can come your way: room upgrades, late checkout, free breakfast and complimentary cocktails.

### BEST DELUXE HOTELS

> Four Seasons Hotel Hong Kong (www.fourseasons.com)
> Grand Hyatt Hotel (www.hongkong.hyatt.com)
> Island Shangri-La (www.shangri-la.com)
> Mandarin Oriental (www.mandarinoriental.com)
> Peninsula Hong Kong (www.peninsula.com)

### BEST BOUTIQUE HOTELS

> Jia (www.jiahongkong.com)
> Hotel LKF (www.hotel-lkf.com.hk)
> The Minden (www.theminden.com)

### BEST FOR STYLE ON A BUDGET

> Bishop Lei International House (www.blshopleihtl.com.hk)
> Ice House (www.icehouse.com.hk)
> Stanford Hillview Hotel (www.stanfordhillview.com)
> The Salisbury (www.ymcahk.org.hk)

### BEST GUESTHOUSES & HOSTELS

> Alisan Guest House (http://home.hkstar.com/~alisangh)
> Booth Lodge (http://boothlodge.salvation.org.hk)
> Hong Kong Hostel (www.wangfathostel.com.hk)
> Rent-a-Room (www.rentaroomhk.com)
> YWCA Building (www.ywca.org.hk)

**Top** Traffic passing a Nathan Rd hotel

# FOOD

The vast majority of Hong Kong's 10,000-odd restaurants serve Chinese food, of course. Cantonese is by far the most popular Chinese cuisine in Hong Kong, but Chiu Chow, Shanghainese, Sichuanese and Northern are also widely available. Cantonese cuisine is famously fresh: there's an emphasis on freshly slaughtered meat (mostly pork and chicken) and seafood. Simple techniques such as steaming and stir-frying allow the ingredients to retain their delicate and well-balanced flavours. Chiu Chow cuisine makes liberal use of garlic, vinegar and sauces; it's famous for goose and seafood dishes. Shanghainese cooking uses a lot of salted and preserved foods and relies on stewing, braising and frying. Sichuanese is the most fiery, making great use of chillies and pungent peppercorns. Northern Chinese food uses a lot of oils (eg sesame and chilli) coupled with ingredients such as vinegar, garlic, spring onions, bean paste and dark soy sauce. Steamed bread, dumplings and noodles are preferred to rice; and lamb and mutton, seldom seen on other Chinese menus, are also popular.

If you're having a bad noodle day, don't despair: Hong Kong is where East eats West and you'll find bangers 'n' mash and lasagne before you can say 'beef tendon *congee*'. Central is the best pick for Western restaurants, especially Soho, though you'll also find a fair few in Tsim Sha Tsui.

## BEST DIM SUM RESTAURANTS
> City Hall Maxim's Palace (p52)
> Lin Heung Tea House (p65)
> Luk Yu Tea House (p65)
> Sweet Dynasty (p123)
> Yung Kee (p66)

## BEST FOR LATE-NIGHT BITES
> 369 Shanghai Restaurant (p87)
> Good Luck Thai Food (p64)
> Tsui Wah (p55)

## BEST...
**For Cantonese** Yung Kee (p66), West Villa (p101)
**For Chiu Chow** Eastern Palace Chiu Chow Restaurant (p120), Leung Hing Restaurant (p55)
**For Shanghainese** Wu Kong Shanghai Restaurant (p123), Yi Jiang Nan (p66)
**For Northern Chinese** Hutong (p121), Spring Deer (p122), Water Margin (p101)
**For Sichuanese** Da Ping Huo (p63), Red Pepper (p100), Shui Hu Ju (p66)
**For international cuisine** Felix (p120), M at the Fringe (p65)

**Opposite** Barbecued ducks in a Wellington St restaurant, Central **Above** Making bean curd with scallops and crab roe

# ARCHITECTURE

SNAPSHOTS

Over the centuries, Hong Kong has played host to everything from Tao temples and Qing dynasty forts to Victorian churches and Edwardian hotels. But Hong Kong's ceaseless cycle of deconstruction and rebuilding means that few structures have survived the wrecking ball. The best places for pre-colonial Chinese architecture still extant are the New Territories and Outlying Islands. Central on Hong Kong Island is good hunting grounds for surviving colonial architecture though Tsim Sha Tsui can boast a few classic examples. Needless to say, enthusiasts of modern architecture will have a field day here. Central and Wan Chai on Hong Kong Island are especially rich showcases for the modern and contemporary buildings.

## BEST CONTROVERSIAL BUILDINGS
> Bank of China Tower (p44)
> Hong Kong Cultural Centre (p126)
> Hongkong & Shanghai Bank (p46)
> Jardine House (p47)
> Two International Finance Centre (p49)

## BEST PRE-COLONIAL CHINESE BUILDINGS
> Kowloon Walled City Park buildings (p138)
> Law Uk Folk Museum buildings (p97)
> Tin Hau Temple (p96)

## BEST COLONIAL BUILDINGS
> Flagstaff House Museum of Tea Ware (p82)
> Former French Mission Building (p45)
> Hong Kong Heritage Discovery Centre (p115)
> Legislative Council Building (p47)
> Murray House (p106)

# DRINKING

Drinking venues in Hong Kong run the whole gamut, ranging from fairly authentic British-style pubs with meat pies, darts and warm beer to stylish lounges where the clothes are straight out of the shopping bag, the sounds are smooth, the drinks are electric and the buzz is hardcore gossip.

Much of Hong Kong's nightlife takes place in top-end hotels, where inventive cocktails, skilled bar staff and some of the best views in town attract both visitors and locals. Overall, Lan Kwai Fong in Central is the best – and most expensive – area for bars, though it's the stomping grounds of expat and Chinese suits, and professionals. The pubs in Wan Chai are cheaper and more relaxed, while those in Tsim Sha Tsui generally more local.

## BEST STYLISH BARS & PUBS
> Bohemian Lounge (p69).
> Champagne Bar (p90)
> Courtney's (p124)
> Dragon-I (p67)
> Maya (p91)

## BEST FOR ONE FOR THE ROAD
> Bar 109 (p90)
> Bit Point (p67)
> Gecko Lounge (p67)
> Mangrove Bar (p124)
> Mes Amis (p91)

## BEST FOR GENEROUS HAPPY HOURS
> Delaney's (p91)
> Devil's Advocate (p91)
> Inn Side Out & East End Brewery (p103)

## BEST FOR MEETING NONPOSERS
> Barco (p67)
> Brecht's Circle (p103)
> Club 71 (p67)

## BEST FOR FRONT-ROW CRUISING
> Bacar (p66)
> Havana (p68)
> Soda (p68)

SNAPSHOTS

# FITNESS & SPORT

Walking and t'ai chi are the most popular physical activities in Hong Kong. Short for *taijiquan* (fist of the supreme ultimate), t'ai chi is a form of slow-motion martial art that has been popular for centuries, especially among older people. The movements develop breathing muscles, promote digestion and improve muscle tone and can also form a solid foundation for any other martial arts practice.

Golf is generally a rich person's sport, undertaken more for networking and prestige than fitness. Tennis and gym sessions are also popular, and most top-end hotels have gyms and pools – some of them quite luxurious. Several fitness club chains in Hong Kong allow short-term memberships for $150 to $200 a day, and both Kowloon Park (p115) and Victoria Park (p97) have swimming pools that are more for leisure than laps.

## BEST HOTEL SWIMMING POOLS

> Empire Hotel Kowloon (www
  .asiastandard.com)
> Grand Hyatt Hotel (www.hongkong
  .hyatt.com)
> Renaissance Harbour View Hotel
  (www.renaissancehotels.com)
> Royal Garden Hotel (www.rghk.com.hk)
> Royal Plaza Hotel (www.royalplaza
  .com.hk)

## BEST...

**Deal for scents** DK Aromatherapy (p70)
**For putting a spring in your step**
Happy Foot Reflexology Centre (p72)
**For cappuccino wraps and other
esoterica** Sense of Touch (p73)
**For a workout** California Fitness (p70),
Yoga Fitness (p73)

# GAY & LESBIAN

The gay scene in Hong Kong has undergone quite a revolution over a few short years. It was only in 1991 that the Crimes (Amendment) Ordinance removed criminal penalties for homosexual acts between consenting adults over the age of 18. Since then gay groups have been lobbying for legislation to address the issue of discrimination on the grounds of sexual orientation. Despite these changes, however, Hong Kong Chinese society remains fairly conservative, and it can still be risky for gays and lesbians to come out to their family members or employers. Be sure to get hold of a copy of the free monthlies *Gmagazine* or the more comprehensive *Q Guide* or log on to **GayStation** (www.gaystation.com.hk) or **Gay Hong Kong** (www.gayhk.com).

**BEST...**
**For cruising** Works (p73)
**For dancing** Propaganda (p72)
**For happy hours and tea dances** Club 97 (p70), FINDS (p63)
**On Kowloon side** New Wally Matt Lounge (p127)

SNAPSHOTS

# KIDS

Hong Kong is a great travel destination for kids, though the crowds, traffic and pollution might be off-putting to some parents. Food and sanitation is of a high standard, and the territory is jam-packed with things to entertain the young 'uns. As a starting point for ideas, get a copy of the HKTB's **Hong Kong Family Fun Guide** (www.discoverhongkong.com /eng/travelneeds/family/mk_fami_maps.jhtml).

Business travellers and tourists alike are bringing their children in increasing numbers to Hong Kong, and many deluxe and top-end hotels, including the Peninsula Hong Kong, the Island Shangri-La and the Mandarin Oriental (p165), have special programmes for children, ranging from art workshops to Chinese cookery lessons.

Children are generally welcome in Hong Kong's restaurants – especially Chinese ones. Few restaurants have highchairs or booster seats, however, so bring your own if you can't do without, or rely on a couple of telephone directories. Though most restaurants don't do special children's servings, Chinese food is generally shared and it's easy to create your own munchkin-sized portion.

Most hotels will be able to recommend babysitters if you have daytime appointments or are considering a night out without the kid(s). Otherwise contact **Rent-a-Mum** ( ☎ 2523 4868; www.rent-a-mum.com; rentamum@netvigator.com) and expect to pay between $110 and $160 per hour.

---

## BEST CHILDREN'S ATTRACTIONS

> Hong Kong Disneyland (p149)
> Ngong Ping Skyrail (p149)
> Ocean Park (p106)
> The Peak (p74)
> Tsim Sha Tsui Promenade (p115)

## BEST...

**For birds and animals** Hong Kong Wetland Park (p144), Yuen Po St Bird Garden (p131), Hong Kong Zoological & Botanical Gardens (p45)

**For educational fun** Hong Kong Heritage Museum (p144), Hong Kong Maritime Museum (p106), Space Museum & Theatre (p113)

**For beaches** Lantau (p148), Repulse Bay (p106)

**For fun transport** Central Escalator (p58), Hong Kong Island's Trams (p195), Star Ferry (p192)

# MACAU

Macau is a dichotomy. On the one hand, the fortresses, churches and food of its former colonial master, Portugal, speak to a uniquely Mediterranean style on the South China Coast. On the other, Macau is the now self-styled Las Vegas of the East, which is why the vast majority of Chinese visit the place. But there is a lot more to Macau than just gambling. The tiny peninsular and the islands of Coloane and Taipa constitute a colourful palette of pastels and ordered greenery. The Portuguese influence is everywhere – cobbled back streets, baroque churches, ancient stone fortresses, Art Deco apartment buildings and restful parks and gardens – and there are several world-class museums. It's well-worth at least a day trip from Hong Kong.

## BEST SIGHTS
> A-Ma Cultural Village (p159)
> Casinos (p158)
> Lou Lim Ioc Garden (p155)
> Macau Museum (p155)
> Ruins of the Church of St Paul (p156)

## BEST PORTUGUESE & MACANESE RESTAURANTS
> A Lorcha (p157)
> Clube Militar de Macau (p157)
> Cozinha Pinócchio (p161)
> Espaço Lisboa (p161)
> Restaurante Litoral (p158)

# MUSEUMS & GALLERIES

Hong Kong boasts some two-dozen museums that are scattered across the territory and explore everything from tea ware and space exploration to horse racing and the history of medicine. At the same time, Hong Kong counts twice as many galleries that show everything from cutting edge home-grown art to old photographs and 'decorative' pieces created to 'blend in'. Some 40 galleries, both commercial and government supported, take part in the annual Hong Kong Art Walk (p29) in March.

## BEST...
**For blockbuster exhibitions** Hong Kong Museum of Art (p112)
**For cutting-edge exhibitions** Para/Site Art Space (p47), Shanghai St Artspace (p130)
**For Chinese culture** Hong Kong Heritage Museum (p144)
Law Uk Folk Museum (p97)

## BEST FOR KIDS
> Hong Kong Maritime Museum (p106)
> Hong Kong Science Museum (p113)
> Hong Kong Space Museum & Theatre (see photo above; p113)

## BEST FOR CONTEMPORARY HONG KONG ART
> Grotto Fine Art (p59)
> Hanart TZ Gallery (p51)

V

# PARKS & GARDENS

Hong Kong has no shortage of parks; indeed, the territory counts almost two dozen country parks (mostly in the New Territories and the Outlying Islands) where you can walk, hike, bird-watch etc. But you don't have to travel great distances in Hong Kong in order to commune with nature; the urban areas of Hong Kong Island and Kowloon are hardly devoid of parks and gardens. Some, such as Hong Kong Park, are laid out to 'reflect' rather than 'represent' nature, and are awash in fake waterfalls and stone 'mountains', while others, such as Hong Kong Wetland Park, embrace Mother Nature with open arms.

**BEST…**
**For art** Kowloon Park (p115)
**For history along with the greenery** Kowloon Walled City Park (p138)
**For museums** Hong Kong Park (p82)
**For t'ai chi practice** Victoria Park (p97)
**For wildlife** Hong Kong Zoological & Botanical Gardens (p45), Hong Kong Wetland Park (see photo above; p144)

# SHOPPING

Hong Kong may not be the bargain basement it once was, but it still wins hands-down in the region for variety and its passionate embrace of competitive consumerism. Any international brand worthy of its logo sets up at least one shop here, and there are a slew of local brands worth spending your money on. Clothing (ready-made or tailored), shoes, jewellery, luggage and, to a lesser degree nowadays, electronic goods are the city's strong suits.

There is no sales taxes (for the moment at least – see p183) so the marked price is the price you'll pay. Credit cards are widely accepted, except in markets. It's rare for traders to accept travellers cheques or foreign currency as payment. Sales assistants in department or chain stores rarely have any leeway to give discounts, but you can try bargaining in owner-operated shops and certainly in markets.

Shops in Central are open from 10am to between 6pm and 7.30pm daily. In Causeway Bay and Wan Chai many will stay open until 9.30pm or 10pm. In Tsim Sha Tsui, Yau Ma Tei and Mong Kok they close around 9pm.

## BEST SHOPS FOR GIFTS & SOUVENIRS

> Chinese Arts & Crafts (p116)
> King & Country (p85)
> Liuligongfang (p51)
> Shanghai Tang (p52)
> Yue Hwa Chinese Products Emporium (p133)

## BEST…

**For antique Chinese furniture** Chine Gallery (p59), Hobbs & Bishops Fine Art (p59)
**For vintage clothing and accessories** Amours Antiques (p58)
**For antique maps and photographs** Wattis Fine Art (p62)

## BEST…

**For men's fashion** Blanc de Chine (p50), Kent & Curwen (p85)
**For women's fashion** Joyce (p51), Vivienne Tam (p85)
**For funky jewellery** Rock Candy (p61)
**For bespoke fashion** Pacific Custom Tailors (p85)
**For street fashion** D-Mop (p98), Spy (p99)

## BEST BOOKSHOPS

> Dymocks Booksellers (p50)
> Kelly & Walsh (p85)
> Kubrick Bookshop (p134)
> Swindon Books (p119)
> Tai Yip Art Book Centre (p61)

# VEGETARIAN

Chinese vegetarian food has undergone a renaissance in recent years, and it is consumed by devout Buddhists and the health-conscious alike. Large monasteries in Hong Kong, including Po Lin on Lantau, often have vegetarian restaurants though you will also find many restaurants in Kowloon and on Hong Kong Island. For the most part they are Cantonese or Shanghainese and strictly vegetarian as they are owned and operated by Buddhists.

You don't have to go to a vegetarian restaurant to find meatless dishes, though. Vegetarian *congee* is available in most noodle shops, and dim sum houses serve a number of vegetarian treats, including *chongyau beng* (onion cakes) and *fu pei gun* (crispy tofu roll).

Western vegetarian food is less easy to come by here if you want anything more complex than a salad, but there are a few options in Central and on Lamma Island. Some Indian restaurants are exclusively vegetarian, but most in Hong Kong offer a combined menu.

**BEST…**
**For vegan food** Life (p64)
**For Shanghainese vegetarian food** Kung Tak Lam (p99)
**For South Indian vegetarian food** Branto Pure Vegetarian Indian Food (p119)
**For vegetarian brunch** Bookworm Café (p150)

# BACKGROUND

## HISTORY

Until the arrival of the British in the early 19th century, Hong Kong was a neglected corner of the Chinese empire inhabited by farmers, fishermen and, on 'remote' islands such as Cheung Chau (p148), pirates. Trade between China and Britain had commenced in around 1685, but the balance was unfavourable to the Europeans – until they began bringing opium into China in the late 18th century.

Despite bans issued by Chinese Emperor Jiaqing and his son and successor, Dao Guang, trade in opium continued until 1839 when the commissioner of Guangzhou, Lin Zexu, destroyed 20,000 chests – almost half a tonne – of the 'foreign mud' at Humen (Taiping). This gave Britain the pretext they needed to take military action against China. British gunboats besieged Guangzhou and then sailed north, forcing the Chinese to negotiate. Captain Charles Elliot, the chief superintendent of trade, demanded that a small, hilly island near the mouth of the Pearl River be ceded 'in perpetuity' to the English crown. Hong Kong formally became a British possession in August 1842.

The so-called Second Anglo-Chinese War (1856–60) won the Kowloon peninsula – and control of Victoria Harbour – for the British. Less than 40 years later, China agreed to lease the much larger 'New Territories' to Britain for a period of 99 years.

Steady numbers of Chinese refugees fleeing war and famine entered the colony from the early 20th century up to the late 1930s. In 1941 Japanese forces swept down from Guangzhou and occupied Hong Kong for four years, imprisoning both local Chinese and foreigners at Stanley Fort.

The communist revolution in China in 1949 sent more refugees pouring into Hong Kong. On a paltry, war-scarred foundation, local and

---

**CONFRONTATION**

'Since May 1967, communist organizations in Hong Kong have sought to impose their will on the government and the people by intimidating workers, fomenting work stoppages, by demonstrations and rioting, and by indiscriminate violence. It has been a testing time for the people of Hong Kong.'

*Hong Kong Yearbook 1967*

---

## HONG KONG IN PRINT

> *Hong Kong: Epilogue to an Empire* (Jan Morris) Anecdotal and very readable history of Hong Kong.
> *Myself a Mandarin* (Austin Coates) Very charming and highly recommended memoirs of a special magistrate in the New Territories of the 1950s.
> *Fragrant Harbour* (John Lancaster) Doorstop novel records seven decades of Hong Kong history through the eyes of four characters.
> *Old Hong Kong* (Formasia) If you like old pictures with your history, this three-volume work is for you.
> *Culture Smart! Hong Kong* (Clare Vickers) An easy and fairly comprehensive introduction to Hong Kong culture.

foreign businesses built an immense manufacturing (notably textiles and garments) and financial services centre that transformed Hong Kong into one of the world's great economic successes. By 1960, Hong Kong was home to about 3 million people, up from a population of 600,000 at the end of the war.

China, having locked itself in its own cage in the 1950s, began rattling it in the following decade. In 1967, at the height of the so-called Cultural Revolution, violent riots provoked by Mao Zedong's ultraleftist Red Guards rocked the colony. Panic spread but Hong Kong stood firm; Chinese Premier Chou Enlai intervened and Hong Kong got on with the business it knew best: making money.

Few people gave much thought to Hong Kong's future until the late 1970s, when the British and Chinese governments started meeting to decide what would happen in (and after) 1997. Though Britain was legally bound to hand back only the New Territories – and not Hong Kong Island and Kowloon, which had been ceded 'in perpetuity' – most of the population lived there; it would have been an untenable division. In December 1984 Britain formally agreed to hand back the entire territory, and a joint declaration affirmed that the 'Hong Kong Special Administrative Region' would retain its social, economic and legal systems for 50 years after the handover.

Nervousness increased as the handover date drew closer, especially after 1989 when Chinese troops mowed down pro-democracy demonstrators in Beijing's Tiananmen Square, and both people and capital moved to safe havens overseas. A belated attempt by Britain to increase the number of democratically elected members of Hong Kong's Legislative Council spurred China to set up a pro-Beijing Provisional Legislative Council across the border in Shenzhen. On 1 July 1997 this body took office in Hong Kong, and Shanghai-born shipping magnate Tung Chee Hwa was named chief executive.

Hong Kong has weathered many storms in the decade since becoming a 'SAR', including a severe economic downturn (below), several outbreaks of deadly Severe Acute Respiratory Syndrome (SARS), and a number of crucial interventions by Chinese authorities in Hong Kong's affairs, including what was seen as the 'upstairs demotion' of Tung, who had been returned for a second five-year term as chief executive in 2002.

# GOVERNMENT & POLITICS

Hong Kong 'constitution' is the Basic Law, published in 1988, which in theory guarantees Hong Kong's freedom in everything except foreign affairs. But Hong Kong does not have what could be called a democratic system, although democratic elements exist within its structure. In effect, business governs the territory, the democratic elements that do exist are limited and the people are, to a large degree, apolitical.

The executive branch of power is led by the chief executive, Donald Tsang, who replaced Tung in 2005. Though he is scarcely more popular than his predecessor, Tsang, who served as financial secretary and was knighted under the *ancien régime,* is at least more credible. And with the economy once again booming, and the withdrawal of Anson Chan, Hong Kong's most popular political figure, from the contest, Tsang was assured re-election in March 2007.

The Hong Kong government has become more executive-led over the past decade, turning the Legislative Council, which debates and passes legislation proposed by the Executive Council, into little more than a rubber-stamp body.

# ECONOMY

Business is Hong Kong's heart and soul. The monopolies in certain sectors of the economy (eg transport and power generation) notwithstanding, the territory remains a capitalist's dream and the most economically free in the world, with trade virtually unrestricted, a hard-working labour force, excellent telecommunications and very low taxes (the maximum personal income tax is 16% while company profits tax is capped at

## DOMESTIC SITUATION

Hong Kong has traditionally suffered from a labour shortage. Most of the menial work (domestic, construction etc) is performed by imported labour, chiefly from Southeast Asia. On Sunday – what they call 'freedom day' – a large percentage of Hong Kong's 156,000 Filipino *amahs* (maids) take over Central's pavements and public spaces, especially pedestrianised Chater Rd and Statue Square. They come in groups to share food, gossip, play cards, do one another's hair and even sing and pray together. The territory's 66,000 Indonesian maids tend to converge on Victoria Park (Map p95) on the same day for picnics and impromptu soccer matches.

17.5%). However, the government is considering the introduction of a controversial general sales tax (VAT) to broaden the narrow tax base.

Service industries now employ about 84% of Hong Kong's workforce and make up 88% of its GDP; the manufacture of textiles, toys and other commodities now takes place over the border. Mainland China supplies almost 43% of Hong Kong's total imports and exports. Other important trading partners are Japan (12%), Taiwan (8%), the USA (7%), South Korea (5%) and Singapore (3%).

The start of the 21st century was a trying time for the Hong Kong economy. Hong Kong maintained an average GDP growth of 5% through the 1990s and peaked at 10% in 2000, but fell to just 0.6% in 2001. Three years later a surge in trade with China and a phenomenal increase of visitors from the mainland saw consumer prices rise (and deflation disappear) for the first time in almost six years. By 2006, unemployment had reached a five-year low of 4.5% and real GDP growth had climbed back to 7.3%. Most importantly, property prices, always viewed as a boom-or-bust gauge here, were at their highest since the handover. Visitors should expect to see general prices rise over the next few years.

# ENVIRONMENT

Pollution has been and remains a major problem in Hong Kong, but it wasn't until 1989, with the formation of the **Environmental Protection Department** (EPD; www.epd.gov.hk), that government authorities acted decisively to clean up the mess. The EPD has had to deal with decades of serious environmental abuse and – almost as serious – a population that until recently didn't know (or care) about the implications of littering and pollution.

---

**WHERE THE GRASS IS GREEN(ER)**

Not all of Hong Kong is ravaged. Some 425 sq km – 38% of the total land area – has been designated as protected country parkland. These 23 parks and 15 'special areas' – for the most part in the New Territories and on the Outlying Islands, but also encompassing the slopes of Hong Kong Island – comprise uplands, woodlands, coastlines, marshes and all of Hong Kong's 17 freshwater reservoirs. In addition, there are four protected marine parks and one marine reserve.

---

Hong Kong's waterways are in a terrible state, but there have been some slight improvements over the past decade. A disposal system in Victoria Harbour is now collecting up to 70% of the sewage there and the *E.coli* count indicating the presence of bacteria has stabilised. The quality of the water at Hong Kong's 43 gazetted beaches must be rated 'good' or 'fair' to allow public use.

Air pollution, responsible for an estimated 15,600 premature deaths a year, is an even more serious concern, especially now that it is hitting Hong Kong where it hurts the most: in its pockets. According to a survey conducted by the American Chamber of Commerce in August 2006, some 40% of senior executives polled said Hong Kong's worsening air quality made it difficult to recruit overseas staff. On the positive side, however, the governments of Hong Kong and Guangdong, where most of the air pollution originates, jointly committed themselves to reducing regional emissions of breathable suspended particulates, nitrogen oxides, sulphur dioxide and volatile organic compounds by more than half by 2010. An hourly update of Hong Kong's air pollution index can be found on the EPD's website.

# SOCIETY & CULTURE

While Hong Kong may seem very Westernised on the surface, Chinese beliefs and traditions persist at every level of society. Buddhism and Taoism – mixed with elements of Confucianism, traditional ancestor worship and animism – are the dominant religions. In general, though, Chinese people are much less concerned with high-minded philosophies than they are with the pursuit of worldly success, the appeasement of spirits and predicting the future. Visits to temples are usually made to ask the gods favours for specific things, such as a loved one's health or the success of a business.

## FENG SHUI

Literally 'wind water', feng shui (or geomancy), aims to balance the elements of nature to create a harmonious environment. It's been in practice since the 12th century, and it continues to influence the design of buildings (p44), highways, parks, tunnels and other sites in Hong Kong. To guard against evil spirits, who can move only in straight lines, doors are often positioned at an angle. For similar reasons, beds cannot face doorways. Ideally, homes and businesses should have a view of calm water (even a fish tank helps). Corporate heads shouldn't have offices that face west: otherwise profits will go in the same direction as the setting sun.

## FORTUNE TELLING

There are any number of props and implements that Chinese people use to predict the future, but the most common method of divination in Hong Kong are *chim* – the 'fortune sticks' (p139) found at Buddhist and Taoist temples.

## NUMEROLOGY

In Cantonese, the word for 'three' sounds similar to 'life', 'nine' like 'eternity' and the ever-popular number 'eight' like 'prosperity'. Lowest on totem pole is 'four', which shares the same pronunciation with the word for 'death'. As a result, the right (or wrong) number can make (or break) a business or relationship. The Bank of China Tower officially opened on 8 August 1988; August is always a busy month for weddings.

## ZODIAC

The Chinese zodiac has 12 signs like the Western one, but their representations are all animals. Your sign is based on the year of your birth

### THE YEAR OF THE...

> **Pig** (2007) Noble, chivalrous, loyal
> **Rat** (2008) Ambitious yet honest
> **Ox** (2009) Bright, patient and inspiring
> **Tiger** (2010) Aggressive, courageous, candid and sensitive
> **Rabbit** (2011) Talented, articulate, affectionate and shy
> **Dragon** (2012) Eccentric, complex, passionate, healthy

(according to the lunar calendar). Being born or married in a particular year is believed to determine one's fortune, so parents often plan for their children's sign. The year of the dragon sees the biggest jump in the birth rate, closely followed by the year of the tiger.

# ARTS

The phrase 'cultural desert' can no longer be used for Hong Kong. There are philharmonic and Chinese orchestras, Chinese and modern dance troupes, a ballet company and several theatre companies. And the number of international arts festivals seems to grow each year.

## CHINESE OPERA

Chinese opera, an unusual hybrid of song, dialogue, mime, acrobatics and dancing, is a world away from the Western variety and many foreigners find it hard to appreciate. Performances can last up to five or six hours, and the audience makes an evening of it – eating, chatting among themselves and playing musical chairs when bored, laughing at the funny parts, crying at the sad bits.

Costumes, props and body language reveal much of the meaning in Chinese opera – check out the enlightening display on Cantonese opera at the Hong Kong Heritage Museum (p144). For a better understanding of this art form join the Cantonese Opera Appreciation Class in the HKTB's 'Meet the People' programme (p113).

## CINEMA

Once the third-largest in the world (after India and the USA), Hong Kong's film industry has gone into freefall in recent years. The days of gravity-defying kung fu fight scenes and Bruce Lee-esque conflict resolution are mostly a thing of the past; a small but productive independent film industry continues to churn out about 100 films each

---

### CATCH IT WHERE YOU CAN

The best time to see and hear Chinese opera is during the Hong Kong Arts Festival (p28) in February or March, and outdoor performances are staged in Victoria Park during the Mid-Autumn Festival (p32). At other times, you might take your chances at catching a performance at the Temple St Night Market (p130) or Hong Kong City Hall (p55).

## NO-NOS & DO-DOS

There aren't many unusual rules of etiquette to follow in Hong Kong; in general, common sense will take you as far as you'll need to go. But on matters of identity, appearance and gift-giving, local people might see things a little differently than you do. For pointers on how to conduct yourself at the table, see p63.

> **Clothing** Beyond the suited realm of business, smart casual dress is acceptable even at swish restaurants. On the beach, topless is a local turn-off and nudity a no-no.

> **Colours** These are often symbolic to Chinese people. Red symbolises good luck, virtue and wealth (though writing in red can convey anger or unfriendliness). White symbolises death, so avoid giving white flowers (except at funerals).

> **Face** Think status and respect (both receiving and showing): keep your cool, be polite, and order a glass of vintage Champagne at an expensive hotel. You've arrived.

> **Gifts** If you want to give flowers, chocolates or wine to someone (a fine idea if invited to their home), they may appear reluctant for fear of seeming greedy, but insist and they'll give in and accept. Money enclosed in little red envelopes (laisee) is given at weddings and the lunar new year.

> **Name Cards** Hong Kong is name-card crazy and in business circles they are a must. People simply won't take you seriously unless you have one (be sure to offer it with *both* hands). Bilingual cards can usually be printed within 24 hours; try printers along Man Wa Lane in Central or ask your hotel to direct you.

year. International hits have included Wong Kar Wai's *In the Mood for Love* (2000) and its follow-up *2046* (2004) as well as the *Infernal Affairs* (2002–03) good cop/bad cop trilogy directed by Andrew Lau-Wai Keung and Alan Mak Siu Fai. The annual Hong Kong International Film Festival in April, now in its third decade, is one of the world's major film festivals.

## DANCE

Hong Kong's professional dance companies are the **Hong Kong Dance Company** (www.hkdance.com), for Chinese traditional and folk, **City Contemporary Dance Company** (www.ccdc.com.hk) and the **Hong Kong Ballet** (www.hkballet .com), for classical and contemporary.

One traditional form of Chinese dance that lives on in Hong Kong is the lion dance. A dance troupe under an elaborately painted Chinese lion costume leaps around to the sound of clanging cymbals, giving the dancers a chance to demonstrate their acrobatic skills.

## MUSIC

Classical music is alive and well here and very popular with local people. The city boasts Chinese, philharmonic and chamber orchestras as well as a sinfonietta. Established overseas performers frequently make it to Hong Kong, especially during February's Hong Kong Arts Festival (p28).

Hong Kong's home-grown popular music scene is known as Canto-pop, a saccharine mix of romantic melodies and lyrics. Rarely radical, the songs invariably deal with such teenage concerns as unrequited love and loneliness. The music is slick and singable, thus the explosion of karaoke parlours. Veteran names in the music industry are thespian/crooner Andy Lau, Jackie Cheung, Faye Wong and Sally Yip. More recent arrivals include Leo Ku, Edmond Leung, Andy Hui and the female duo Twins.

## PAINTING

Painting in Hong Kong falls into three broad categories: contemporary local, classical Chinese and classical Western. Contemporary local art differs from that of mainland China, as Hong Kong artists are largely the offspring of refugees and the products of a cultural fusion; they blend East and West and are concerned with finding their orientation in the metropolis through personal statement. The best places to see examples of this art are at the Hong Kong Museum of Art (p112), Hanart TZ Gallery (p51) and Para/Site Art Space (p47).

## THEATRE

Nearly all theatre here is Western in form and staged in Cantonese. Theatre groups include the **Hong Kong Repertory Theatre** (www.hkrep.com) and the more experimental **Chung Ying Theatre Company** (www.chungying.com).

# DIRECTORY
## TRANSPORT
### ARRIVAL & DEPARTURE

Most international travellers arrive and depart via Hong Kong International Airport.

Travellers to and from mainland China can use ferry, road or rail links (below) to Guangdong and points beyond. Hong Kong can be reached from Macau via ferry or helicopter.

### AIR

Sleek **Hong Kong International Airport** (Map p147, B5; www.hkairport .com) is on Chek Lap Kok, an island flattened and extended by reclaimed land off the northern coast of Lantau Island. Check-in is on level seven; departures level six.

Highways, bridges (including the 2.2km-long Tsing Ma Bridge) and a fast train on 34km of track link the airport with Kowloon and Hong Kong Island.

## Information

**Airport Hotline** ( ☎ 2181 0000; www .hkairport.com)
**Hotel Booking Service** ( ☎ 2383 8380, 2769 8822; www.hkha.org)
**Left Luggage** ( ☎ 2261 0110)
**Air Canada** ( ☎ 2867 8111; www .aircanada.ca)
**Air New Zealand** ( ☎ 2862 8988; www .airnewzealand.com.hk)
**British Airways** ( ☎ 2822 9000; www .ba.com)
**Cathay Pacific** ( ☎ 2747 1888; www .cathaypacific.com)
**Oasis Hong Kong Airlines** ( ☎ 3628 0628; www.oasishongkong.com)
**Qantas** ( ☎ 2822 9000; www.qantas .com.au)
**United Airlines** ( ☎ 2810 4888; www .unitedairlines.com.hk)
**Virgin Atlantic Airways** ( ☎ 2532 6060; www.virgin-atlantic.com)

## Airport Access

The **Airport Express** ( ☎ 2881 8888; www.mtr.com.hk) departs from Hong Kong station ($100) in Central every 12 minutes from 5.50am to 12.48am daily, calling at Kowloon

---

### OTHER WAYS TO GO

As noted in the introduction to this chapter, you don't have to take to the skies to reach Hong Kong – at least from the north (China) and the west (Macau). Travellers to/from mainland China make use of ferries, buses and trains. Indeed, the celebrated Trans-Mongolian and Trans-Manchurian trains will get you from Beijing to Moscow while very much on the ground; contact **Monkey Shrine** (www.monkeyshrine.com) or **Russia Experience** (www.trans-siberian.co.uk) for details. It's also possible to drive or take a bus to Macau and then catch a ferry to Hong Kong from there.

## Local Travel Box

| | Central | Peak | Causeway Bay |
|---|---|---|---|
| Central | n/a | 🚡 Peak, 10min | Ⓜ Island line, 6min |
| Peak | 🚡 Peak, 10min | n/a | Ⓜ Island line, 6min & 🚡 Peak, 10min |
| Causeway Bay | Ⓜ Island line, 6min | Ⓜ Island line, 6min & 🚡 Peak, 10min | n/a |
| Tsim Sha Tsui | Ⓜ Tsuen Wan line, 5min | Ⓜ MTR Tsuen Wan line, 5min & Peak | Ⓜ Island & Tsuen Wan lines, 8min |
| Sha Tin | Ⓜ Island line, 6min & 🚆 KCR East Rail, 16min | Ⓜ Island line, 6min, 🚆 KCR East Rail, 16min & 🚡 Peak, 10min | 🚌 170, 50min |
| Lantau | 🚠 Lantau, 31–48min | 🚠 Lantau, 31–48min & 🚡 Peak, 10min | Ⓜ Island line, 8min & 🚠 Lantau, 31–48min |

station ($90) in Jordan and at Tsing Yi Island ($60) en route; the full trip takes 24 minutes. Vending machines dispense tickets at the airport and train stations en route. You can also use an Octopus card (p195).

Major hotel and guesthouse areas on Hong Kong Island are served by buses A11 ($40) and A12 ($45); the A21 ($33) does similar areas in Kowloon. Buses run every 10 to 30 minutes from 6am to between midnight and 1am; the 'N' buses follow the same route after that. Buy tickets at the booth near the airport bus stand.

A taxi from the airport to Tsim Sha Tsui/Central costs $270/340.

**Parklane Limousine Service** ( ☎ 2261 0303; www.hongkonglimo.com) and **Trans-Island Limousine Service** ( ☎ 2261 2155; www.trans-island.com.hk) charge $450/550 to the same destination for up to four people.

## BUS
Several transport companies in Hong Kong offer buses to Guangzhou, Shenzhen airport and other destinations in the Pearl River Delta:
**CTS Express Coach** ( ☎ 2365 0118, 2261 2472; http://ctsbus.hkcts.com)
**Eternal East** ( ☎ 3412 6677, 2261 0176; www.eebus.com)
**Gogobus** ( ☎ 2375 0099, 2261 0886; www.gogobus.com)

| Tsim Sha Tsui | Sha Tin | Lantau |
|---|---|---|
| (M) Tsuen Wan line, 5min | 182, 1hr | Lantau, 31–48min |
| (M) Tsuen Wan line, 5min & Peak, 10min | 182, 1hr & Peak, 10min | Lantau, 31–48min & Peak, 10min |
| (M) Island & Tsuen Wan lines, 8min | 170, 50min | (M) Island line, 8min & Lantau, 31–48min |
| n/a | KCR East Rail, 16min & Lantau, 31–48min, Sat & Sun 35min | (M) Tsuen Wan line, 5min |
| KCR East Rail, 16min | n/a | Lantau, 31–48min & 182, 1hr |
| (M) Tsuen Wan line, 5min & Lantau, 31–48min, on weekends Lantau, 35min | Lantau, 31–48min & 182, 1hr | n/a |

**Motor Transport Company of Guangdong & Hong Kong** ( ☎ 2375 2991, 2317 7900; www.gdhkmtc.com).

## BOAT

Services to/from Macau run round-the-clock. Boats depart from the Macau ferry terminal (Map p43, A4) in Sheung Wan, and the China ferry terminal (Map p111, B6), Kowloon. Tickets ($142 from Hong Kong Island, $140 from Kowloon, higher prices from about 6pm to 6am and weekends) can be bought at the terminals or by calling carriers **Turbojet** ( ☎ 2859 3333; www.turbojet.com.hk) or **New World First Ferry** ( ☎ 2131 8181; www.nwff.com .hk). Jet catamarans and hovercraft also leave both terminals (though primarily the China ferry terminal) to destinations in Guangdong.

## DEPARTURE TAX

The Hong Kong airport departure tax ($120 for everyone over 12 years) is almost always included in the price of the ticket.

## TRAIN

To get to/from Shenzhen in mainland China, just board the Kowloon–Canton Railway's East Rail (KCR; p194) at Hung Hom (Map p111, A1) or East Tsim Sha Tsui stations and ride it for 40 minutes to Lo Wu ($33/66 for 2nd/1st class); Shenzhen 200 metres away.

The **Kooloon-Guangzhou express train** (www.kcrc.com) departs from the Hung Hom station a dozen times daily (from $180, 1¾ hours). Tickets can be booked in advance at KCR stations in Hung Hom, Kowloon Tong and Sha Tin; from China Travel Service (CTS) agents; or over the phone through the **Intercity Passenger Services Hotline** ( ☎ 2947 7888).

Another rail line links Kowloon with both Shanghai and Beijing. Trains to Beijing (hard/soft sleeper from $547/934, 24 hours) via Guangzhou, Changsha and Wuhan, leave on alternate days. Trains to Shanghai ($508/825, 23 hours) via Guangzhou and Hangzhou leave on the other days.

## TRAVEL DOCUMENTS
### Return/Onward Ticket
Visitors requiring visas have to show that they have adequate funds for their stay (a credit card should do the trick) and that they hold an onward or return ticket.

### Visa
Visas are not required for citizens of the UK (up to 180 days), of other European Union (EU) countries, Australia, Canada, Israel, Japan, New Zealand and the USA (90 days) and South Africa (30 days). Others should check visa regulations

(www.immd.gov.hk/ehtml/hkvi sas_4.htm) before leaving home.

## GETTING AROUND
Hong Kong is small and crowded, and public transport is the only practical way to move people.

The ultramodern Mass Transit Railway (MTR) subway is the quickest way to get to most urban destinations. The bus system is extensive and as efficient as the traffic allows, but it can be bewildering for short-term travellers. Ferries are fast and economical and throw in spectacular harbour views at no extra cost. Trams are really just for fun.

In this guide we include icons – MTR, bus, train/tram or ferry – to indicate the most practical and convenient form of transport for each listing.

In this book, the nearest Metro, bus, train/tram or ferry route is noted after the Ⓜ , 🚌 , 🚆 or 🚢 in each listing. See also the transport map on the inside back cover.

## BOAT
There are four Star Ferry routes, but by far the most popular is the one running between its new home in Central (outlying islands ferry terminal pier 7; Map p43, F1) and Tsim Sha Tsui (Map p111, D5). Fares are $1.70/2.20 (lower/upper deck) and, frankly, there's no other

trip like it in the world. Star Ferries also links Central with Hung Hom; and Wan Chai with Hung Hom and Tsim Sha Tsui.

Three other ferry companies operate cross-harbour routes but the only one of real interest to travellers is the hydrofoil from Queen's Pier (Map p43, F3) in Central to Tsim Sha Tsui East (adult/child $4.60/2.30). Two separate ferry companies operate services to the outlying islands, including Lantau, Cheung Chau and Lamma, from ferry terminal piers 4, 5 and 6 (Map p43, E1) in Central.

## BUS

Hong Kong's extensive bus system will take you just about anywhere in the territory. Most buses run from 5.30am or 6am until midnight or 12.30am, though there are a handful of night buses that run from 12.45am to 5am or later. Bus fares cost from $2.40 to $45, depending on the destination, with night buses costing $12.80 to $31. You will need exact change or an Octopus card (p195).

Central's most important terminal for buses is below Exchange Square (p44). From here you can catch buses to Aberdeen, Repulse Bay, Stanley and other destinations on the southern side of Hong Kong Island. In Kowloon, the Star Ferry bus terminal (Map p111, D5) has buses heading up Nathan Rd and to the Hung Hom train station.

Figuring out which bus you want can be difficult although it's useful to know that any bus number ending with the letter M (eg 40M) goes to an MTR station and that buses with an X are express ones.

## Minibuses

Also known as 'public light buses' (an official term that no-one ever uses in conversation), minibuses seat up to 16. Small red minibuses ($2 to $20) don't run regular routes; you can get on or off unless restricted by road rules. Green 'maxicabs' operate on some 350 set routes and make designated stops. Two popular routes are the 6 ($4.50) from Hankow Rd in Tsim Sha Tsui to Tsim Sha Tsui East and Hung Hom station in Kowloon, and the 1 ($8) to Victoria Peak from next to Hong Kong station.

## CAR & MOTORCYCLE

It would be sheer madness for a newcomer to consider driving in Hong Kong. Traffic is heavy, the roads can get hopelessly clogged and finding a parking space is difficult and very expensive.

If you do need to hire a vehicle, hire one with driver from **Ace Hire Car** (☎ 2572 7663, 2893 0541; www.acehirecar .com.hk), which has chauffeur-driven cars for $160 to $250 per hour (minimum two to five hours, depending on location).

## TAXI

Hong Kong taxis are a bargain compared to cabs in other world-class cities. The flag fall for taxis on Hong Kong Island and Kowloon is $15 for the first 2km and $1.40 for every additional 200m. It's slightly less in the New Territories ($12.50/1.20) and on Lantau Island ($12/1.20).

## TRAIN

### Kowloon–Canton Railway

**Kowloon–Canton Railway** (KCR; ☎ 2929 3399; www.kcrc.com) consists of two lines: KCR East Rail, which runs from East Tsim Sha Tsui station to Lo Wu on the mainland border, and the newer KCR West Rail, which links Nam Cheong station in Sham Shui Po (New Kowloon) with Tuen Mun in the New Territories. The KCR is the fastest way to get up to the New Territories. The 30-minute rides to Sheung Shui on the East Rail and Tuen Mun on the West Rail, for example, cost just $12.50 and $15 respectively.

### Mass Transit Railway

The **MTR** ( ☎ 2881 8888; www.mtr .com.hk) is clean, fast and safe and transports around 2.4 million people daily. Tickets cost $4 to $26

---

### NEED TO KNOW

**Electricity** The standard voltage is 220V, 50Hz AC. Most electric outlets are designed to accommodate the British variety with three square pins.

**Metric System** The metric system is official use, but traditional Chinese weights and measures persist at local markets, including *leung* (37.8g) and *gan* (catty; about 605g). There are 16 *leung* to the *gan*.

**Newspapers & Magazines** The local English-language newspapers are the **South China Morning Post** (www.scmp.com) published daily ($7), and the **Hong Kong Standard** (www.thestandard.com.hk) Monday to Saturday ($6). The Beijing mouthpiece **China Daily** (www.chinadaily.com.cn) prints a Hong Kong English–language edition ($6). The *Asian Wall Street Journal* as well as regional editions of *USA Today*, the *International Herald Tribune* and the *Financial Times* are printed in Hong Kong.

**Radio** Popular English-language stations in Hong Kong are RTHK Radio 3 (current affairs and talkback; 567AM, 1584AM, 97.9FM and 106.8FM), RTHK Radio 4 (classical music; 97.6FM-98.9FM), RTHK Radio 6 (BBC World Service relays; 675AM), AM 864 (hit parade; 864AM) and Metro Plus (news; 1044AM).

**Television** The two English-language terrestrial stations are TVB Pearl and ATV World.

**Time** Hong Kong Standard Time is eight hours ahead of GMT; there is no daylight-savings time in summer.

($3.80 to $23.10 if purchased with an Octopus card). Trains run every two to 10 minutes from around 6am to between 12.30am and 1am daily on six lines including the Airport Express line. Ticket machines accept notes and coins and dispense change.

## TRAM

Hong Kong Island's double-decker trams are not fast but are fun, cheap and a great way to explore the northern coast. For a flat fare of $2 (dropped in a box beside the driver as you disembark) you can rattle along as far as you like over 16km of track, 3km of which winds its way into Happy Valley. Trams operate from around 6am to as late as 12.30am and run every two to 10 minutes.

The six routes (west to east) are: Kennedy Town–Western Market, Kennedy Town–Happy Valley, Kennedy Town–Causeway Bay, Sai Ying Pun (Whitty St)–North Point, Sheung Wan (Western Market)–Shau Kei Wan and Happy Valley–Shau Kei Wan. The longest run (Kennedy Town–Shau Kei Wan, with a change at Western Market) takes about 1½ hours.

Strictly speaking a funicular, the Peak Tram (one-way/return adult $22/33, senior and child 3 to 11 years $8/15) departs for Victoria Peak about every 10 to 15 minutes from 7am to midnight. The tram's lower **terminus** (Map p43, D2; 33 Garden Rd, Central) is behind St John's Building, at the northwestern corner of Hong Kong Park.

## TRAVEL PASSES

The **Octopus card** ( ☎ 2929 3399; www.octopuscards.com), a rechargeable 'smart card' valid on most forms of public transport in Hong Kong, costs $150. This includes a $50 refundable deposit and $100 worth of travel. Octopus fares are between 5% and 10% cheaper than ordinary ones on the MTR and KCR.

For shorter stays there's the new **Tourist MTR 1-Day Pass** ($50), valid on the MTR for 24 hours after the first use.

# PRACTICALITIES
## BUSINESS HOURS

Business hours are 9am to 5.30pm or 6pm Monday to Friday and (sometimes) 9am to noon or 1pm on Saturday. Many offices close for lunch between 1pm and 2pm.

Shops catering to tourist trade keep longer hours, but almost nothing opens before 9am, and many stores don't open until 10am or 10.30am. Even tourist-related businesses shut down by 10pm.

Most banks, post offices, shops and attractions are closed on public holidays; restaurants usually open daily, including Sunday.

## CLIMATE & WHEN TO GO

October, November and nearly all of December are the best months to visit. Temperatures are moderate, the skies are clear and the sun shines. January and February are cloudy and cold but dry. It's warmer from March to May but the humidity is high, with lots of fog and drizzle. The sweltering heat and humidity from June to September can make for some sweaty sightseeing; the threat of typhoon looms throughout September.

Travel in and out of Hong Kong can be especially difficult during Chinese New Year (late January/early February).

## DISCOUNTS

Children aged three to 11 and seniors over 60 or 65 are generally offered half-price admission at attractions and on most forms of transport, but family tickets are rare. The Hong Kong Museums Pass (p76) Is worth considering.

### STUDENT, YOUTH & TEACHER CARDS

The International Student Identity Card (ISIC) offers discounts on some forms of transport and cheaper admission to museums and other attractions. If you're under 26 but not a student, you can apply for an International Youth Travel Card (IYTC) issued by the Federation of International Youth Travel Organisations (FIYTO), which gives much the same discounts. Teachers can apply for the International Teacher Identity Card (ITIC).

## EMERGENCIES

Hong Kong is generally very safe both night and day but, as with anywhere, things can go wrong.
**Ambulance, Fire & Police** ☎ 999
**Police (crime hotline)** ☎ 2527 7177
**Rape Crisis Line** ☎ 2375 5322

## HOLIDAYS

**New Year's Day** 1 January
**Chinese New Year** Three days in late January/early February
**Easter** Four days in late March/April
**Ching Ming** Early April
**Buddha's Birthday** Late April/May
**Labour Day** 1 May
**Dragon Boat Festival** Late May/June
**Hong Kong SAR Establishment Day** 1 July
**Mid-Autumn Festival** Late September/October
**China National Day** 1 and 2 October
**Cheung Yeung** October
**Christmas Day** 25 December
**Boxing Day** 26 December

## INTERNET

### INTERNET CAFÉS

With the plethora of places offering low-cost or free wi-fi, including most hotels, all of Hong Kong International Airport (p189), the Peak Cafe Bar (p68) in Soho and

Cafe Deco (p78) on the Peak, you'll have no trouble accessing the internet with your own laptop. If you don't bring yours along, Hong Kong has plenty of independent options:

**Central Library** (Map p95, D3; ☎ 3150 1234, 2921 0500; www.hkpl.gov.hk; 66 Causeway Rd, Causeway Bay; ☽ 10am-9pm Thu-Tue, 1-9pm Wed) Free access.

**Pacific Coffee Company** (Map p43, C3; ☎ 2537 1688; www.pacificcoffee.com; ground fl, The Work Station 43 Lyndhurst Tce, Central; ☽ 7am-midnight Mon-Thu, 7am-1am Fri & Sat, 8am-11pm Sun) Free access with purchase; one of scores of branches in Hong Kong.

**Shadowman Cyber Cafe** (Map p111, C4; ☎ 2366 5262; shadowmancybercafe@yahoo .com.hk; ground fl, Karlock Bldg, 21A Ashley Rd, Tsim Sha Tsui; h8am-midnight Mon-Thu, 8am-1am Sat, 10am-midnight Sun) First 20 minutes free with purchase, then $10 every 15 minutes.

## INTERNET RESOURCES

**LonelyPlanet.com** (www.lonelyplanet .com) is a good start for many of Hong Kong's more useful links.

**Hong Kong Information Services Department** (www.info.gov.hk)

**Hong Kong News.Net** (www.hongkong news.net)

**Hong Kong Observatory** (www.weather .org.hk)

**Hong Kong Outdoors** (www.hkoutdoors .com)

**Hong Kong Telephone Directory** (www .pccw.com)

**Hong Kong Tourism Board** (www.discover hongkong.com)

**South China Morning Post** (www.scmp .com.hk)

## LANGUAGE

Cantonese and English are Hong Kong's two official languages. While Cantonese is used in Hong Kong in everyday life by most (some 94%) of the population, English is still the primary language of commerce, banking, international trade and the higher courts.

However, there has been a dramatic rise in the number of Mandarin-speaking tourists since the handover, and some locals are now learning Mandarin in preference to English.

### BASICS

| | |
|---|---|
| Hello, how are you? | *nei ho ma?* |
| Goodbye. | *baai baai/joi gin* |
| I'm fine. | *ngo gei ho* |
| Excuse me | *m goi* |
| Yes. | *hai* |
| No. | *m hai* |
| Thank you very much. | *do je saai/m goi saai* |
| You're welcome. | *m sai haak hei* |
| Do you speak English? | *nei sik m sik gong ying man a?* |
| I don't understand. | *ngo m ming* |

### EATING & DRINKING

| | |
|---|---|
| That was delicious. | *jan ho mei* |
| I'm a vegetarian. | *ngo hai sik jaai ge* |
| The bill, please. | *m goi, maai daan* |

| roast pork | char siu |
| barbecued pork with rice | char siu fan |
| roast duck | char siu ngap |
| roast goose | char siu ngoh |
| fried rice | chau fan |
| fried noodles | chau min |
| braised mixed vegetables | lo hon tsai |

## SHOPPING

| How much is this? | ni go gei do chin a? |
| That's too expensive! | taai gwai laa! |

## EMERGENCIES

| I'm sick. | ngo yau beng |
| Help! | gau meng a! |
| Call the police! | giu ging chaat! |
| Call an ambulance! | giu gau seung che! |
| Call a doctor! | giu yi sang! |

## TIME & NUMBERS

| today | gam yat |
| tomorrow | ting yat |
| yesterday | kam yat |

| 0 | ling |
| 1 | yat |
| 2 | yi (leung) |
| 3 | saam |
| 4 | sei |
| 5 | ng |
| 6 | luk |
| 7 | chat |
| 8 | baat |
| 9 | gau |
| 10 | sap |
| 11 | sap yat |
| 12 | sap yi |
| 20 | yi sap |

| 21 | yi sap yat |
| 100 | yat baak |
| 101 | yat baak ling yat |
| 110 | yat baak yat sap |
| 120 | yat baak yi sap |
| 200 | yi baak |
| 1000 | yat chin |

## MONEY

### ATMS
International travellers can withdraw funds from their home accounts using just about any of the numerous ATMs scattered around the territory.

### COSTS
Hong Kong is a relatively pricey destination. You can survive on $250 a day, but it will require a good deal of self-discipline. It's better to budget something along the lines of $400 for midrange options.

### CREDIT CARDS
The most widely accepted cards are Visa, MasterCard, American Express, Diners Club and JCB. When signing credit card receipts, write 'HK' in front of the dollar sign. For 24-hour card cancellations or assistance, try the following:

**American Express** ( ☎ 2811 6122)
**Diners Club** ( ☎ 2860 1888)
**JCB** ( ☎ 2366 7211, 2877 5280)
**MasterCard** ( ☎ 800 966 677)
**Visa** ( ☎ 800 900 782)

## CURRENCY

The local currency is the Hong Kong dollar (HK$). The dollar is divided into 100 cents. Notes are issued in denominations of $10, $20, $50, $100, $500 and $1000. There are coins of 10c, 20c, 50c, $1, $2, $5 and $10.

## ORGANISED TOURS

Tourism is one of Hong Kong's biggest money-spinners, so it's no surprise that there is a mind-boggling array of tours available via every conceivable conveyance. Some of the best tours are offered by the **Hong Kong Tourist Board** (HKTB; ☎ 2508 1234; www.discoverhongkong .com), and tours run by individual companies can usually be booked at any HKTB branch (p200). Some of the more unusual tours include the horse racing. If you know nothing about it but would like to attend a meeting, consider joining the Come Horseracing tour available through **Splendid Tours & Travel** ( ☎ 2316 2151; www.splendid tours.com) during the racing season. The tour ($580, except at 10 special and cup meetings when it is $630 to $1080) includes admission to the Visitors' Box of the Hong Kong Jockey Club Members' Enclosures and buffet with drinks. Tours scheduled at night (Wednesday) last about 5½ hours, while daytime tours

(Saturday or Sunday) are about seven hours long.

For more animal interaction, try a scenic dolphin-spotting expedition in a four-hour tour ($320/160) off Lantau Island offered by **Hong Kong Dolphinwatch** ( ☎ 2984 1414; www .hkdolphinwatch.com; 15th fl, Middle Block, 1528A Star House, 3 Salisbury Rd, Tsim Sha Tsui), which includes information on the plight of the endangered Chinese white dolphin – between 100 and 200 inhabit Hong Kong's coastal waters. Departures are at 8.30am from City Hall in Central and at 9am from the Kowloon Hotel in Tsim Sha Tsui every Wednesday, Friday and Sunday.

The HKTB invites visitors on a free one-hour ride two days a week on a sailing junk called the **Duk Ling**. Boarding is at 2pm and 4pm on Thursday and 10am and noon on Saturday at the Tsim Sha Tsui Public Pier next to the Star Ferry terminal (Map p111, D5) in Tsim Sha Tsui. Visitors should register with any HKTB branch in advance.

**Kayak and Hike** ( ☎ 9300 5197; www .kayak-and-hike.com) offer a fabulous four-hour tour of the harbour around Sai Kung in the New Territories, taking you by unique 'fast pursuit craft' (FPC) to the otherwise inaccessible Bluff Island and the small fishing village of Leung Shuen Wan. The tour price ($700)

DIRECTORY

includes Chinese lunch as well as snorkelling gear. Tours depart from Sai Kung pier at 10am (9am on Sunday); book in advance.

Learn all about t'ai chi, feng shui and Chinese tea in a four-hour tour ($298/248) from **Sky Bird Travel** ( ☎ 2369 9628; www.skybird.com .hk). Tours depart at 7.30am from the Excelsior Hong Kong Hotel in Causeway Bay and at 7.45am from The Salisbury YMCA in Tsim Sha Tsui on Monday, Wednesday and Friday.

An unusual way of touring Hong Kong with a 'guide' is on offer from **Walk the Talk** ( ☎ 2380 7756; www.walkthetalk.hk), effectively an audioguide that uses your own mobile phone. For $80, you get a guided tour of Hong Kong's most popular neighbourhoods with snappy commentary, anecdotes and tales of old Hong Kong. There are also WAP and 3G versions for those wanting to see pictures of places as they were 50 or even 100 years ago. The packages, which include maps and a 100-page booklet, are available from HKTB branches and selected bookshops.

## PHOTOGRAPHY & VIDEO

Any photographic accessory you could possibly need is available in Hong Kong. Stanley St (Map p43, C3) on Hong Kong Island is the place to look for reputable camera stores; Photo Scientific (p61) is especially recommended.

## TELEPHONE

All local calls in Hong Kong are free except at public payphones, where they cost $1 for five minutes.

### MOBILE PHONES

Hong Kong boasts the world's highest per-capita usage of mobile telephones and pagers, and they work everywhere – even in tunnels and the MTR. Any GSM-compatible phone can be used in Hong Kong.

Retail outlets **PCCW** ( ☎ 2888 288; www.pccw.com) and **Hong Kong CSL** ( ☎ 2888 1010; www.hkcsl.com) rent and sell mobile phones, SIM cards and phone accessories. Handsets can be rented from $35 per day, and rechargeable SIM chips cost $180/280 for 293/600 minutes. Top-up cards will set you back $100, $200 and $500.

### PHONECARDS

International direct-dial (IDD) calls can be made to almost anywhere in the world from public phones with a phonecard. These are stored-value Hello cards in denominations of $50 to $500, available at 7-Eleven and Circle K convenience stores, Mannings pharmacies and Wellcome supermarkets.

## USEFUL PHONE NUMBERS

**Local directory inquiries** ☎ 1081
**International directory inquiries** ☎ 10015
**International access code** ☎ 001
**Reverse-charge (collect)** ☎ 10010
**International credit card** ☎ 10011
**Time & air temperature** ☎ 18501

## TIPPING

Hong Kong is not very tip conscious; taxi drivers only expect you to round up to the nearest dollar. Tip hotel staff $10 to $20, and if you use porters at the airport, $2 to $5 a suitcase is expected. Most hotels and many restaurants add 10% service charge to the bill.

## TOURIST INFORMATION

The efficient and friendly **Hong Kong Tourism Board** (HKTB; www.discoverhong kong.com) produces reams of useful pamphlets. Its website is also a good point of reference.

There are HKTB branches at **Hong Kong International Airport** (Map p147, B5; ☺ 7am-11pm), the **Star Ferry Concourse** (Map p111, D5; ☺ 8am-8pm) in Tsim Sha Tsui, and near Exit F of the Causeway Bay MTR station (Map p95, B3; ☺ 8am-8pm). Alternatively, you can try calling the **HKTB Visitor Hotline** ( ☎ 2508 1234; ☺ 8am-6pm).

## TRAVELLERS WITH DISABILITIES

Disabled people will have to cope with MTR and KCR stairs as well as pedestrian overpasses, narrow footpaths and steep hills. People whose sight or hearing is impaired must be cautious of Hong Kong's demon drivers. On the other hand, some buses are now accessible by wheelchair, taxis are never hard to find and most buildings have lifts (many with Braille panels). Wheelchairs can negotiate the lower decks of most of the ferries, and almost all public toilets now have access for the disabled.

Contact the **Joint Council for the Physically and Mentally Disabled** (Map p81, C4; ☎ 2864 2931; fax 2865 4916; Room 1204, 12th fl, Duke of Windsor Social Service Bldg, 15 Hennessy Rd, Wan Chai).

# >INDEX

*See also separate indexes for See (p211), Shop (p213), Eat (p214), Drink (p215) and Play (p216).*

INDEX

**000** map pages

**000** map pages

## SEE

**000** map pages

# EAT

**Brazilian**
Boi na Brasa 157

**Café**
Flying Pan 63
Kubrick Bookshop Cafe 134

**Cantonese**
Che's Cantonese Restaurant 87-8
Dong 120
Lin Heung Tea House 65
Ming Court 135
One Harbour Road 88
Sweet Dynasty 123
Tai Woo 79
Tsui Wah 55
West Villa 101
Yung Kee 66

**Chinese**
American Restaurant 87
Beijing Shui Jiao Wong 87
Rainbow Seafood Restaurant 150
Saint's Alp Teahouse 135
Tai Ping Koon 100
Top Deck at the Jumbo 109
Tung Kee Seafood Restaurant 145

**Chinese, Northern**
Hutong 121
Peking Restaurant 135
Spring Deer 122
Water Margin 101
Yi Jiang Nan 66

**000** map pages

**Chiu Chow**
Carrianna Chiu Chow Restaurant 87
Eastern Palace Chiu Chow Restaurant 120
Leung Hing Restaurant 55

**Dim Sum**
City Hall Maxim's Palace 52
Luk Yu Tea House 65

**Fast Food**
City'Super 52
Mido 134-5

**French**
2 Sardines 62
Chez Patrick 63
Orphée 100
Petrus 88
W's Entrecote 103

**Hunanese**
Hunan Garden 52

**Ice Cream**
XTC Gelato 123

**Indian**
Bombay Dreams 62
Koh-I-Noor 145
Gaylord 121

**Indonesian**
Indonesian Restaurant 1968 121

**International**
Boathouse 108
Cafe Deco 78

Café Too 87
Eating Plus 78
Felix 120-1
Gogo Café 99
Jaspa's 145
Lucy's 108
M at the Fringe 53, 65
Opia 100
Pearl on the Peak 79
Phoenix 79
R66 88
Stoep 150
Tai Ping Koon 100
Verandah 109

**Italian**
Aqua 119
Fat Angelo's 120
Rugheta 65-6
Sabatini 122
Wildfire 123

**Japanese**
Aqua 119
Go Sushi 99
Kyozasa 121
Sushi One 123
WasabiSabi 100

**Korean**
Arirang 99
Chang Won Korean Restaurant 120
Korea House 54

**Macanese**
Cozinha Pinócchio 161
Fat Siu Lau 158
Restaurante Litoral 158